LIVING
in the **LIGHT** *of*
ETERNITY

Other Books by K. P. Yohannan

Revolution in World Missions
The Road to Reality
Why the World Waits

LIVING
in the LIGHT *of*
ETERNITY

Your Life Can Make a Difference

K. P. Yohannan

Chosen Books

A Division of Baker Book House Co
Grand Rapids, Michigan 49516

© 1995 by K. P. Yohannan

Published by Chosen Books
a division of Baker Book House Company
P.O. Box 6287, Grand Rapids, MI 49516-6287
All rights reserved.

Sixth printing, January 1999

Printed in the United States of America

Library of Congress Cataloging-in-Publication Data

Yohannan, K. P.
  Living in the light of eternity / K. P. Yohannan.
    p.   cm.
  ISBN 0-8007-9235-1 (paper)
  1. Christian life. I.Title.
  BV4501.2.Y6   1995
  248.4—dc20   95-20992

For current information about all releases from Baker Book House, visit our web site:

http://www.bakerbooks.com

This book is dedicated to the staff of Gospel for Asia all around the world. These brothers and sisters share my vision and burden for the lost of Asia. They have sacrificed much in order to serve the native missionaries and enable them to win millions to Jesus.

Contents

Acknowledgments

This book is the result of more than ten years of traveling and speaking to God's people from all walks of life. What you read in this volume has been used by God to change the lives of many. I am grateful to the Lord for allowing me to have a part in touching these lives for the sake of His Kingdom.

This project would not have been possible without the help of my secretary, Heidi Chupp. With tireless determination she typed and proofread the manuscript, added words to make things clear, corrected my spelling and grammar and arranged the chapters in logical order. She did all this and much more without a word of complaint.

I also want to thank Debi Carroll for helping to transcribe the majority of these messages from tapes.

Finally I want to thank my family—my wife, Gisela, and my children, Daniel and Sarah—for their love and support, without which it would be impossible to stay in the battle. They stand with me in our commitment to reach this generation for the Lord.

Introduction

Recently I found myself in an interesting conversation—with my pen! It was a bit one-sided, but I learned some things from that talk.

For as long as I can remember, even in my school days, I have always used a fountain pen. The one I own today is a gift from a friend—a nice pen that I enjoy using.

One day as I sat alone at my desk writing, I looked at that pen in my hand and began a conversation.

"Pen," I said, "I really like you. I think you're the finest thing there is. I don't even loan you out to anyone."

Well, thank you, I imagined the pen to respond. *It's nice to know I'm appreciated.*

"Pen," I continued, "you are really part of my personality. My signature—part of who I am—has been shaped by you. There is something about you that no one else can claim. But I'm sad to tell you, Pen, that after a few years you will no longer be mine."

What do you mean? my pen asked. *Are you planning to give me away?*

"I'm more than forty years old," I explained. "If I added a hundred years to my life, I can't imagine I would be around anymore. You might be, but I'll be gone. So, Pen, I'll use you as long as I can. But I'll not hold you so tightly that I'll have to weep over you when the end comes."

As you begin to read through this book, I challenge you to take a fresh look at how you are investing your life—your time, your energy, your abilities. You have only one life. It is your choice (whether you realize it or not) how you invest it. Will you spend it on yourself and your own pleasures or throw yourself at the feet of Jesus and tell Him, "Here I am—send me"?

When you live your life in the light of eternity, the treasures the world values become worthless. Things do not matter anymore; souls become precious.

It is the prayer of my heart that as you come to the end of this book, you will not close it and say simply, "Well, that was challenging," then go on with your life the way it was before.

Take some time right now to pray and ask the Lord to use this book to soften your heart, fill your eyes with tears and move you out of your comfort zone and into a world that is lost and dying without Jesus Christ.

I challenge you to get beyond the "I've-heard-it-before" mentality. Move into the uncertainty of seeking the will of God for every step. It will be the beginning of a serious, honest walk with Jesus. I can assure you, a life spent in this way will be eternally worth it.

May the Lord bless you and speak to you as you read these pages.

K. P. Yohannan
Carrollton, Texas

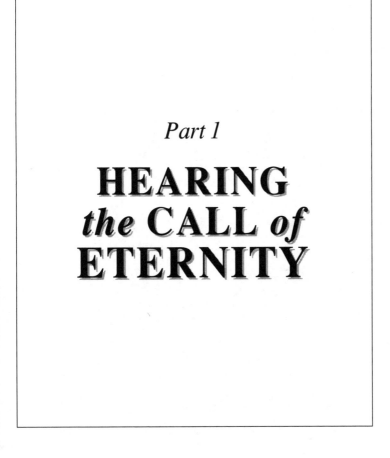

Part 1

HEARING *the* CALL *of* ETERNITY

Lift Up
Your Eyes

What do you consider to be the rock-bottom essentials of life? Let's make some mental notes of the things we need to survive, or just to get by.

Let's start with a house. How many rooms do we need to survive? All right, let's choose a one-bedroom house. Let's add a tiny bathroom; that should be enough. But what about a kitchen? Perhaps a small one. Refrigerator? Can hardly live without it! We will need running water, too—at least cold, and maybe we can add hot as well.

What about electricity? We absolutely need that. Carpeting? Well, it does get cold in the winter. What about a TV? We need to know what is going on in the world.

Let's move on to the car. What kind do we need? A small, domestic-made car will be the cheapest. We should also consider a motorcycle or bicycle—cheaper still.

How about clothes? We are not talking about what we *want*, remember, but only the essentials. A few skirts or pairs of pants, a couple of shirts, some socks or stockings and underclothes will do. Shoes? We can get by with one pair.

Personal care—do we need all those shampoos and conditioners? A bar of soap and a toothbrush will do just fine. Let's also include some deodorant. Perhaps we can add a mirror, but let's keep it small.

Our list is far from finished. What happens when we have a headache? We had better keep some aspirin on hand. Oh, and don't forget the vitamins and Band-Aids.

How about financial security? Well, we should have a small bank account with a few dollars in it.

We do not want to forget the children. They need a few items of clothing, too, and perhaps some toys to keep them busy.

Now let's look over our mental list and think carefully about what we have included. What *does* it take to live? The list we have drawn up is pretty sparse. But in your mind's eye light a match. Hold it to the list. Watch it burn until all that is left is a wisp of ash.

We do not need *any* of these things, however basic they may be, to live. Millions of people in the world who live and die on the streets of New York, Rio, Bombay, Mexico City and elsewhere sleep in cardboard huts, under bridges and in cement sewer pipes. They get by without any of the essentials on our list.

We, too, whether we like it or not, can live without any of these things. There are just two things we absolutely cannot live without: a glass of water and a piece of bread.

Not long ago, while driving in India with several brothers from Gospel for Asia, I noticed something strange in the ditch on the side of the road. A closer look revealed a man lying there motionless.

I thought he was dead. But the driver of the car said as we drove by, "That man has been lying there for six days now."

"What?" I exclaimed. "Tell me what happened."

"He's an old beggar and has been living on the streets. Six nights ago he was hit by a car and must have broken his leg. No one wants to pick him up or even touch him. But an old lady comes every day and gives him some rice and a drink of water."

I was stunned. "If Jesus were to go by this place, what would He do?" I asked.

All of us in the car fell silent.

When we arrived at our destination, I suggested we go to the police and ask for permission to pick up the old man and take him to the hospital. It was granted, and some of our brothers went to get him. They told me the rest of the story later.

The old man's hair looked as though it had never been washed, combed or even cut. He had probably not washed his body in years. The rags he was wearing were black with grime. Thousands of ants, the kind that feed on dead bodies, were eating away at his flesh. Since he had not been able to move since he was hit, he had lain there in his own filth.

At the hospital the nurses tried to remove his clothes to give him a bath, but he kept fighting them. He clutched the rags he wore and would not let go. Finally someone discovered that at one corner of his shirt there was a knot, and in the knot was a one-rupee coin (equivalent to about five cents). He was holding onto this rag for dear life because he did not want to lose his rupee! Once they handed him his coin, he relaxed and let go of his clothes.

As he got better, I went to the hospital several times to visit and pray with him. I learned his story. His name was Kuttappan. He was 75, and for as long as he could remember he had lived on the streets. They were his home. He had no knowledge of relatives, wife, children or home.

Now let me ask you a question: Did Kuttappan survive 75 years without our list of essentials? Yes, he did. As he lay unmoving on the street, only a handful of rice and a glass of water from an old woman kept him alive.

We, too, could survive just as Kuttappan did. In fact, we would do all right without *any* of our "essentials." If we lived in a tropical climate, we could even survive without a stitch of clothing (although perhaps not in public!). But there is no way we could live without bread and water.

Do you find anything in life that carries greater value than these most basic of essentials—something of higher priority than even a piece of bread and a glass of water?

Jesus did. Let's look at John 4 to remind ourselves what was more important to Him than eating and drinking.

A Heart for the Harvest

As we read through the Gospels and observe Jesus' life, we find that He took every opportunity to teach His disciples about the Kingdom of God. And whatever He taught, He lived before them. Everything He said was clearly reflected in His life. He was a living, breathing example to His disciples. These twelve men had an opportunity to watch His life and learn from His every action.

One of the occasions that challenged and changed them is recorded in John 4. It is as relevant for us today as it was for Jesus' disciples. You are probably familiar with the story of the woman at the well to whom Jesus spoke about living water. The disciples had gone into the city to buy food, and when they returned they offered it to Him.

> But he said to them, "I have food to eat that you know nothing about."
> Then his disciples said to each other, "Could someone have brought him food?"

"My food," said Jesus, "is to do the will of him who sent me and to finish his work. Do you not say, 'Four months more and then the harvest'? I tell you, open your eyes and look at the fields! They are ripe for harvest."

John 4:32–35

Can't you identify with the disciples' confusion? Jesus had to be hungry from His journey, so they had walked to the nearby village to buy Him something to eat. They had not eaten yet, either, and were probably just as hungry and thirsty as Jesus was. Then Jesus acted as if He had already eaten: "I have food to eat that you aren't aware of." This confused them even more: "We go to all this trouble and now He won't eat! Has someone brought Him something?"

What was Jesus saying? He was seizing on an everyday event—eating—to illustrate to His disciples a principle of a different Kingdom. Jesus was saying something like this:

"You're horizontally oriented, thinking about the here-and-now—your tired and dusty feet, your growling stomachs, your parched throats. But pull your attention away for a minute. Lift up your eyes! Look into eternity and see what I see. You say there are still four months before harvest arrives. But I tell you, look right now to the souls of men and women around you. The fields are already ripe and ready to be harvested. If you wait a little longer, the crop will be gone—destroyed.

"Yes, I'm hungry, I'm thirsty. But the crisis out there is so real that it consumes all My being. Compared to what is happening, I no longer have an appetite. I am desperate to finish what My Father has given Me to do."

Jesus could have used any number of examples to explain Kingdom principles. Why did He use food?

Perhaps because it makes more sense to us. For us the barest of necessities do not consist of only a glass of water and a piece of bread. Yet to Jesus, even the most basic of essentials—bread and water—were unimportant when He knew people were dying without His Father's love.

Jesus speaks to us today just as strongly as He did to His disciples. He gives us the same command He gave them: "Follow Me." If we are His followers, we will hear this command and do the same things He did. But as human beings, made of the same flesh and blood as Jesus' disciples, we are horizontally oriented, too. We focus on the here-and-now—clothes, houses, educations, careers, bank accounts, finances, cars.

But Jesus calls us to lift our eyes and look away from it all. He is calling us to see what He sees, to feel the urgency He feels, to share His heart for the harvest that will soon be gone—destroyed forever—if it is not reaped soon.

Throughout the Gospel accounts, Jesus' life was marked by urgency: "I must go"; "I must work"; "Night is coming"; "You go and make disciples." Phrases like these tell us how Jesus felt and what He lived for. He was so desperate that food and drink took a back seat.

What a contrast with our casual, laid-back approach to life and our attitude toward the lost world!

Thinking in the Light of Eternity

Newspapers in India carried the story recently of a Hindu man who, like many other devotees, embarked on a pilgrimage to a holy site to receive forgiveness for his sins. His desperate desire to be cleansed of sin caught the eye of the media.

The man had begun his journey with his two sons about 125 miles from the holy mountain that was his destination. He took a small pebble in his hand and lay down on the dirt road, stretching his arm as far as he could reach and putting the pebble there. Then he raised himself up and walked to where the pebble lay. Picking it up, he went through the entire motion again—and again and again.

Body length by body length, he and his sons made their painstaking way to the pilgrimage site.

At one point along a busy highway, a speeding truck hit one of his sons, killing him instantly. But the pilgrim continued on his way, his passion for forgiveness greater than the grief he felt for his son.

"Nothing is too great a price to pay for my forgiveness," he told the news reporters who had gathered at the scene. "I am willing to do whatever it takes."

The man and his remaining son continued on their arduous journey until they finally reached the peak of the holy mountain. As they prepared to offer their sacrifice to the gods they worshiped, the man directed his son to turn away and begin to pray. The boy complied. While he was looking the other way, his father lifted a knife and sacrificed this remaining son in final hope of forgiveness for his sins.

A missionary leader told me later, "That man and his sons passed by on the road beside my house. If I had seen them, I could have given them a tract and shared the Gospel with them. Tell me, how can I *not* be desperate to reach my own people with the Gospel?"

His question has echoed in my mind many times since, especially as I read about events taking place in the world. Since the breakup of the Soviet Union, for example, doors are opening for the Gospel to reach some of her remotest regions. Some of the new republics are nearly one hundred percent Muslim. Who will hear the call of God and win them to Jesus? They all need to be reached with the Gospel—the Uzbeks, the Turkmens, the Azeris and millions of others.

The underground Church is coming forward, willing to send hundreds of young people well-schooled in suffering to go and preach the Gospel full-time. One of the leaders I have been in contact with has told me our prayers and support are urgently needed to reap a harvest of souls that is ripe *today*.

But the average Christian struggles to apply these facts personally. It is easier for us to spend our time and money on ourselves. A wife, realizing her husband's birthday is coming up, shops for something nice for him. She spots a silk tie and thinks, *Oh, that's a handsome one! That'll look nice on him.* She picks it up and takes it over to the cash register without even noticing the twenty-dollar pricetag— one more tie to add to the dozens already in his closet. Yet what do we do with information from the mission field about the needy men and women laying their lives down to reach the unreached with the Gospel? Sometimes we do not want to incorporate these facts into our everyday lives, or we do not know how.

We must lift up our eyes. We need to retrain our minds to interpret everything we do, everything we see, everything we spend in the light of eternity—in the light of souls that are dying without Jesus.

One of the things I learned on my first trip to China still boggles my mind—that there are multitudes of churches there with hundreds, even a thousand, members without a single Bible in the entire congregation. That twenty-dollar tie—do you know it could purchase twenty Bibles, or twenty *thousand* Gospel tracts? Add to this the fact that half the world is still waiting to see the first page of a Bible or even any Gospel literature.

Getting Real

In one of our Gospel for Asia board meetings recently, the members of the board brought up the need for a safer car for my wife, Gisela. Given the vital role she plays in the ministry, both in North America and abroad, they felt we should invest in a well-built foreign model that had some wonderful safety features.

I thought Gisela, who grew up in Germany around expensive European cars, might see the wisdom of this suggestion. But she did not.

"Even if I were to ride in a tank," she replied, "that wouldn't stop an accident from happening. And when I think about our brothers on the mission field who don't even own a bicycle and have to walk ten, fifteen, twenty miles to preach the Gospel, I don't feel comfortable buying an expensive car—even a used one. I don't want it. We'll live with the car we have. It's good enough."

Her reply should not have surprised me.

As I share my heart with you in this chapter, I do not want you to come away with the thought that you have simply read another application of John 4. Please do something about what you are reading! This is where lifting your eyes and hearing the call of eternity truly begins.

We are called to fulfill different tasks in the Lord's Kingdom. Our responses to His call, therefore, will be as individual as we are. Some may hear the call to full-time missionary work. Others may sense the Lord directing them to pray for and send others. Some may make small changes in their lifestyles; others may undergo a radical *coup d'état* of the heart.

Such was the case with a man who phoned me early one morning, awakening me out of a sound sleep.

"I'm sorry to wake you, Brother K. P.," he said.

"It's no problem," I assured him sleepily. "Please tell me what's on your heart."

"I didn't sleep at all last night." Then his voice broke. I could hear him sobbing.

Finally he continued, "I want you to know a little about me. I live very well. I own my own business. I drive two Mercedes. My house is worth three quarters of a million dollars."

He went on listing the valuable things he owned.

"I'm a born-again, Bible-believing Christian who goes to a fine church. But I just finished reading your first book, and I'm so torn up inside that I don't know what to do with myself. I want to be real for the first time in my life. I want to be able to live with myself.

"Just before I called you, I was on my knees before the Lord. I've decided that I'm going to sell my house and purchase a smaller one. After all, it's only me, my wife and our one child. I've decided to sell my two cars and buy something less expensive. And I'm going to sell my fifteen-thousand-dollar watch and get a cheaper one."

He went on and on, listing the changes he wanted to make in his lifestyle.

"I'm glad you called me," I told him. "I pray that as the Lord has spoken to you about making all these changes, they will not be only a little anesthesia to keep you happy for a while, but that you will go the distance in obedience to Him."

Then I prayed with him. And that was the end of our conversation.

A few months later I met a close friend of his.

"How is he doing?" I asked.

"You wouldn't believe it if you saw it. He's sold everything! He is happily living a much simpler life and sharing with everyone why he's done it."

You may say to yourself, "Well, he was rich, and I'm not. Besides, he had a lot of things to get rid of."

My friend, lifting your eyes from the things of this world is an activity that must begin *where you are*. Kuttappan, the old man who lay on the street for six days, was clutching his ragged piece of clothing for dear life. He would not let the filthy thing go. Why? Because he did not want to lose his only coin.

What are you grabbing for? Whether it is a luxury or an essential, nothing is more important to God's heart than reaching the lost. Lift up your eyes, if just for a moment. Ask the Lord to lay His burden on your heart. Ask to share His perspective. See eternity stretching out before you.

Do you see any of the world's riches around the throne of God? No. Rather, you see multitudes—men, women and children that no one can number (Revelation 7:9). Remember, millions of souls from every nation, tribe, people and language are still waiting to find out how they can come before the throne of God. We must keep that vision of eternity before us and live our lives accordingly.

Jesus died for us that we may live. If we choose, we can lift our eyes, see the harvest and live for others that they, too, may hear that He died for them.

This is no pie-in-the-sky spirituality. We have real-life examples to offer us guidance as to how, in our twentieth-century world, we can actually do this.

Living for Another Kingdom

In northeast India a group of tribal people numbers well over eighty thousand. Traditionally the members of that tribe are animists, making sacrifices, worshiping nature and their ancestors. As far as anyone knew, a church had never been established among these people. They lived in spiritual darkness—until a man named Anil heard a Gospel radio broadcast.

Anil had been sent out by the tribe as a boy to get an education. Now, as a young husband and father, he was listening to his radio one day when he heard a name he had never heard before: Jesus Christ. The voice went on to say that Jesus was God who became a Man and died for sinners to save them.

Anil was curious and decided to send a letter to the address given at the end of the program.

"I heard on the radio about Jesus Christ being God," he wrote. "Can you send me a book about your God?"

A few weeks later a New Testament arrived for Anil, which he started reading every day. As he read he grew

26

more and more astounded. *How is it that this took place in history, yet we know nothing about it?* he asked himself.

Since Anil was young and had no authority in the community, he went to speak to the elders.

"I've received this book," he told them. "It tells about a God named Jesus Christ."

He told them what he had been reading and submitted the New Testament to them. The elders were interested. They decided Anil should come every day and read this book to them. He began in Matthew with the genealogy of Jesus but became so confused that he skipped to Matthew 5 and started there.

Every day Anil met with the elders and together they read a few pages out of the New Testament. Within six months the elders were grasping a new concept: Here was a loving God who had died for them but now was dead no longer. This God asked them to live for Him—but in return, He said He would live through them.

The Holy Spirit worked in their hearts one by one, drawing them to Himself. The people of this tribe began to pray to Jesus. They had never heard of the Four Spiritual Laws but were coming to a knowledge of the Lord Jesus and gaining a relationship with Him. Within a year about two hundred people had come to faith in Christ.

Through Anil's reading, meanwhile, the elders learned about baptism. Since they wanted to understand what it was all about, they sent Anil to find someone who could tell them more. Anil had to travel almost twenty miles, asking around, until he found an elderly man who was a missionary in the area.

"We are some people who read your Bible," Anil explained. "We believe in Jesus and pray to Him. Now we've read about baptism. Could you tell us more about this and baptize us?"

Because the old missionary was unable physically to travel twenty miles to baptize these new believers, Anil went home to talk to the tribal elders. They decided to send fifty to sixty believers at a time so the missionary could baptize them. About three hundred believers were baptized in this way.

Then the elders gave Anil another important mission.

"When you were a boy," they told him, "we sent you out to learn to read and write, to become educated. You are the hope and future of our tribe. Now, Anil, you must go someplace where you can learn more about this God, and then return and tell us."

Anil had heard about a ministry in India that trained young people, so he wrote them, requesting to be part of their training program. He never mentioned that he was married and had a child. He longed for the training and wanted nothing to interfere with it. Nor did he tell them about the conversion of his tribe.

Soon a letter arrived telling Anil he was accepted for their year-long training program and could come right away.

During his year with the team, Anil soaked up as much as he possibly could. But he kept his identity a secret until one night during a prayer meeting, when he began to pour out his heart to the Lord for his people. The leaders looked at one another curiously. Was it possible Anil was part of that unreached tribe in northeast India?

Afterward they asked him. Then Anil astounded them with a description of the great move of God among his people. They went to see for themselves and found a radiant, born-again, baptized group in that remote region.

Today there is a thriving, growing church there. Hundreds are coming to Christ and being baptized. Dozens of young people from the tribe are ready to go into full-time ministry to serve the Lord. The entire community has been transformed by the Word of God.

"Come, Follow Me"

Anil and his fellow tribal believers are examples of Christians who have lifted their eyes, seen the fields and are devoting their lives to the harvest. (We will see another contemporary example in chapter 4.) The Holy Spirit touches the hearts of people who commit their lives to Him wholly; who follow Jesus simply because He said, "Follow Me"; and who do whatever He asks them to do. It is as simple as that.

We see the same response from the disciples Jesus called:

> As Jesus walked beside the Sea of Galilee, he saw Simon and his brother Andrew casting a net into the lake, for they were fishermen. "Come, follow me," Jesus said, "and I will make you fishers of men." At once they left their nets and followed him.
>
> When he had gone a little farther, he saw James son of Zebedee and his brother John in a boat, preparing their nets. Without delay he called them, and they left their father Zebedee in the boat with the hired men and followed him.
>
> Mark 1:16–20

These men dropped everything they were doing and followed Jesus. I imagine that Zebedee, James and John's father, watched in consternation as his sons got up from their nets and followed Jesus. Perhaps he called after them. Perhaps he thought they had lost their senses.

But Jesus was saying, "You could spend the rest of your lives catching fish. But if you come and follow Me, I will make you fishers of men."

Jesus still issues that call to those who claim to be His followers.

Peter states, "To this you were called, because Christ suffered for you, leaving you an example, that you should follow in his steps" (1 Peter 2:21).

Jesus told His disciples, "A new command I give you: Love one another. . . . All men will know that you are my disciples if you love one another" (John 13:34–35).

When we read straight through the four Gospels, we can see clearly how Jesus lived His life. It is summed up in this statement: "The Son of Man did not come to be served, but to serve, and to give his life as a ransom for many" (Matthew 20:28).

"My purpose is not for Myself," Jesus was saying, "so that everyone can gather around and take good care of Me. No, I have come as the poorest of the poor. I have come to suffer and die for others."

I remember a story I heard once about William Booth, the founder of the Salvation Army. At the time he was an old, weak man. He was expected to speak at a huge convention, but because of his physical condition he was unable at the last minute to go. Instead he sent a telegram.

Thousands gathered at the convention, eager to hear this great man of God speak. That night, at the appointed moment, someone came to the platform with the sealed telegram and explained that General Booth was unable to be there, but that he had sent a message to be read. As he opened the seal, the crowd grew hushed in expectancy.

There was only one word in the telegram: "Others."

What was Booth saying to them? "Remember, while you hold this great convention and enjoy the food, fellowship and laughter—remember, my message is still unchanged: Others."

If we are followers of Jesus, if we are to hear the call of God, this mindset must govern all of our thinking. We must, like Jesus, be others-centered.

Learning from His Life—and Death

Jesus did not train His disciples in a classroom; He taught them through example. He lived His life before them and then willingly laid it down. No wonder that, after the disciples were filled with the Holy Spirit, they remembered Jesus' words to go into all the world and preach the Gospel. And every one of them laid down his life for preaching the Gospel.

At one time I thought John was the only disciple who was not martyred. Later I learned that he was beheaded. Another disciple, Thomas, is said to have journeyed to India, where he preached and laid down his life for Jesus. One of the seven churches he planted is located about three miles from where I was born and reared.

Doesn't it seem strange that these men who walked and lived with Jesus for three years, men who saw miracles almost beyond belief and who must have had great faith, were not supernaturally translated to heaven, but died criminals' deaths? How could they have traveled to places and done things they knew would put their very lives at risk?

Because Jesus was their example. Jesus was never the kind of Master who told them, "Do what I say, don't do what I do." No, He said, "Come, follow Me."

Jesus also said, "I tell you the truth, anyone who has faith in me will do what I have been doing. He will do even greater things than these, because I am going to the Father" (John 14:12).

I remember studying the book of Acts in Bible college. As we went through it, I thought it was a fascinating piece of history. But it is much more than history. The book of Acts is a living, open-ended book whose story continues even today in the lives of committed believers. It is a book filled with the stories of people who were absolutely sold out, who had only one thing on their minds: Jesus died, He rose again, He is our Lord, He is coming back and we must tell our generation!

These believers yielded their lives unselfishly to communicate this message. When they were misunderstood, mistreated, persecuted, stoned and beaten up, they did not go around mourning their losses and licking their wounds. They went right back out and preached the Gospel—and not just the apostles, but the believers, the everyday, "normal" people like you and me.

When we read about Jesus' life and are challenged to follow in His footsteps, we feel overwhelmed. *I can't help it,* we rationalize. *I'm only a human being. Jesus is God. How can I expect to keep up with Him?* And we excuse ourselves from total commitment.

Then we come to Paul. It is not easy to write Paul off because he was just as human as we are. "I know that nothing good lives in me, that is, in my sinful nature," he wrote in Romans 7:18. He considered himself an earthen vessel, a jar of clay (see 2 Corinthians 4:7).

Paul recognized that in his own strength he started from zero. He confessed his weaknesses and inadequacies continually. This is a man who argued with Barnabas, his coworker. Acts 15:39 tells us that "they had such a sharp disagreement that they parted company." But for this normal human being named Paul, following Jesus was not a nine-to-five job, nor did it have a finishing point. This was everyday life for him.

Let's look at an incident that took place in Paul's life when he came to Thessalonica:

> The Jews were jealous; so they rounded up some bad characters from the marketplace, formed a mob and started a riot in the city. They rushed to Jason's house in search of

Paul and Silas in order to bring them out to the crowd. But when they did not find them, they dragged Jason and some other brothers before the city officials, shouting: "These men who have caused trouble all over the world have now come here. . . ."

Acts 17:5–6

This incident was just one of many for Paul, an everyday occurrence in his Christian walk. He was accused by the crowd of, in the words of the King James Version, having "turned the world upside down." But to him this was simply part of following Jesus.

There was no dichotomy in Paul's life or in the lives of the early believers. Their lives were not compartmentalized into "spiritual" and "secular" activities. Their whole existence was a solid commitment, a life given for the Lord and His Kingdom.

We Know Too Much

Unfortunately most modern-day Christians seem satisfied with only *knowing* what these New Testament believers did. We neglect to follow the example they provide.

The curse on our lives as modern Christians is that we have carefully divided the spiritual from the secular parts of our lives. On certain days we feel holy and wonderful. Our emotions are elevated and we feel ready to face any trial that may come. We are going to conquer the world for the Lord! On other days, back on the job and in the world, we say to ourselves, *How can I do all that for the Lord? I'm doing the best I can.*

Somehow we have become comfortable with living a divided life. When we read about the uproar over Paul in Thessalonica, we have a difficult time relating to the treatment the believers received.

But for those New Testament believers, *normal, everyday living for Jesus brought on persecution.* These people lived in a community and worked faithfully at their jobs every day. Nothing about them stood out, except the fact that they took the words of Jesus seriously and they followed Him.

The reason these believers lived was not to sew tents, teach school or construct buildings. These activities were simply their means of making a living. But their lives did not stop when no one bought tents anymore, when they retired or when they were too exhausted to lay another brick. While these believers lived on earth, their occupations were temporal, insignificant compared to what they saw as their primary responsibility. They lived for another Kingdom.

It is as if the first-century believers were living in the midst of a whirlwind. Wherever they went they caused some kind of commotion or turmoil or trouble—simply because they lived what they believed.

We do *not* read passages like this in the book of Acts:

And they gathered together for the committee meeting, ten people with long faces drinking black coffee with no sugar because they all were watching their diets.

And one spoke up, saying, "Brothers and sisters, God is telling us we should do such-and-such."

Yet another responded, "I'm not sure. We should think about it some more. We're so much in debt right now, maybe we should vote on it."

So it goes in the lives of countless churches today. We are so intent on finding the hidden meanings behind the mandates in the New Testament that we forget to look at the mandates themselves. We are so organized that we make it difficult for the Holy Spirit to direct and use us to change the world around us.

We find no committee meetings in the book of Acts. We find long hours of prayer, fasting and waiting on God to move. The believers of Acts were common people like us, but wherever they went, things happened. As these men and women moved out into the marketplace, into their neighborhoods and workplaces, they turned their communities upside-down. They were revolutionaries who had heard the call of God.

Look at Jesus' life. He was a revolutionary, too. Wherever He went, nothing stayed the same. He saw the darkness, the condition of the lost, and it drove His life.

This is how the Lord wants us to live as well—as world revolutionaries who cannot help but change the world around us because of what we hear and see.

The call of Christ rings in our ears: "Follow Me, and I will make you fishers of men." Jesus is not playing games with us. And hell is no joke; hell is real. I tell you, if we examine ourselves and discover that we really do not believe what we claim to believe, we might as well get out of this business. But if we *do* believe what we say we believe, let's be different. We cannot live for ourselves anymore; we have been given too much knowledge for that. And from those to whom much is given, much will be required (see Luke 12:48).

Let's think carefully and plan deliberately to live our lives in such a way that they *will* make a difference.

The question is, how do we do that? How do we live our lives as world revolutionaries?

Revolutionized from Within

The small island nation of Sri Lanka, located off the southeastern tip of India, was in the throes of civil war for a decade. Tens of thousands of innocent people were butchered as two separate races fought for what they both believed was rightfully theirs. These groups were involved in terrorist, guerrilla-type warfare, ruthless in their attacks and committed to their cause.

Countless Sri Lankans fled the island and the violence, seeking refuge in India. Many native missionaries ministered to these refugees, who lost literally everything in order to escape with their lives. On one of my visits to a refugee camp in the early 1990s, my eyes were opened to the horrible reality of what war could do. I saw ten-by-twelve-foot rooms with bare concrete walls, no cooling or heating, no running water, no windows and only a door for ventilation and light. I saw thirty or more people crammed into each room. I honestly do not know how a person can survive in those conditions.

As we went from room to room, the missionary pointed out certain people to me: "That man is a medical doctor. His wife and children were killed. See him? He's a lawyer. That one over there is a teacher. . . ."

I looked around and saw men and women who had lived in the upper class of their society, now brought to ruin by the war. The doctor sat in a corner wearing the only piece of clothing he owned; he was dirty, unshaven and looked depressed. I am sure he was dreaming of his wife and children, lamenting that they were no longer with him.

Who killed the people? Who drove them out? Terrorists so bent on achieving their goal that they would stop at nothing, ready even to die for their cause. I am told that many of them carried a cyanide pill for use if they were captured by their enemies. I read in an Indian newspaper that thirty to forty of these terrorists died in one month's time. They were caught and arrested but committed suicide before anyone could gather any information.

Recently I read about the recruiting practices of one of the groups. Four or five members would drive a jeep into a remote but populous part of the country and set up loudspeakers in the public market that blared out their message to the people. Finally, when a large crowd had gathered, the group would make an announcement like the following:

"We challenge you young people to come forward and give your lives for this cause. We challenge you parents to give up your sons. We challenge you mothers to offer your children for our people, and you will remember forever a people who laid down their lives for the future of our nation."

I can scarcely believe this, but I read in the article that young people would step forward, and mothers pushed their thirteen- and fourteen-year-old sons forward, saying, "Go, go!" Then the group would load the recruits into the jeep and drive off, never to be seen again.

What kind of creatures *are* these people? People committed to a kingdom here on earth—a kingdom that will eventually totter and perish. But their commitment gives us part of the answer to the question we asked in the last chapter: How do we live as world revolutionaries?

Living Out the Embarrassing Implications

The guerrillas from Sri Lanka demonstrate the first of three principles I offer to help us become radical revolutionaries who have heard the call of God: *We must live according to what we know, committed to a heavenly Kingdom, so that our lives affect not only our home and community, and perhaps our state and country—but the entire earth.*

My son Daniel has always been fascinated with how things work. One of his favorite things to do is to take something apart and tinker with it. He is always inventing, or reinventing, some little gadget. One of his attempts as a young boy was reinventing firecrackers. He would break the heads off some matches, roll them up in paper and light it, hoping for an explosion.

I never did see one of those "firecrackers" actually explode. On the outside each one looked like a firecracker, but it did not act like one. Why not? Because what Daniel rolled up lacked the explosive charge of a true firecracker.

We said in the last chapter that we know too much. We know about the Gospel but we do not give ourselves to its life-changing implications. Knowledge brings responsibility. Implementing our knowledge of the Gospel is not easy, but it does no good for us to look right on the outside but lack true power within. Just like Daniel's firecrackers, we will be duds.

The Bible is full of illustrations of two groups of people—those who know the truth and say, "Lord, Lord," but who demonstrate by their very lives that they do not really mean it; and those who say, "Lord, Lord," and follow His footsteps. The second group are the people who have counted the cost, who look straight at the cross and gladly accept the inconveniences, pain and price they must pay to follow the Lord.

We read about these people of faith in Hebrews 11. Their faith cost them everything but they changed the course of their generation. C. S. Lewis wrote in *The Screwtape Letters*, "Active habits are strengthened by repetition but passive ones are weakened. The more often [a man] feels without acting, the less he will be able ever to act, and in the long run, the less he will be able to feel."

How true this is! God's Word says, "Do not merely listen to the word, and so deceive yourselves. Do what it says" (James 1:22).

A. W. Tozer wrote in his book *The Root of the Righteous*:

We can prove our faith by our committal to it, and in no other way. Any faith that does not command the one who holds it is not a real belief; it is a pseudo belief only. And it might shock some of us profoundly if we were brought suddenly face to face with our beliefs and forced to test them in the fires of practical living.

Many of us Christians have become extremely skillful in arranging our lives so as to admit the truth of Christianity without being embarrassed by its implications.

So wide is the gulf that separates theory from practice in the church that an inquiring stranger who chances upon both would scarcely dream that there was any relation between them. An intelligent observer of our human scene who heard the Sunday morning sermon, and later watched the Sunday afternoon conduct of those who had heard it, would conclude that he had been examining two distinct and contrary religions.

Christians habitually weep and pray over beautiful truth, only to draw back from that same truth when it comes to the difficult job of putting it in practice.

When we hear the New Testament with willing, open hearts, the Gospel will penetrate our very lives and break them open, energizing our eyes, our ears, our hands, our legs—every part of us. And when we allow the Gospel to energize us, we become vessels in the Lord's hands, pouring out our prayers, finances, reputation, lifestyle—and ultimately our very lives.

Superstars Need Not Apply

Do we have to be "somebody" to hear the call of God and make a difference? In my own life I have seen time and again how God uses "nobodies." Sometimes I feel insecure. At other times I feel overwhelmed with all that I know needs to be done. Again and again I struggle and fail.

Where do I go when this happens? To the cross! How many times? Many times a day, if needed. The cross is the place where I can go and say, "Lord, I am Yours, along with all my weaknesses. But Your grace alone is what I need to serve You."

Perhaps you feel you are useless to the Lord, that you are not good enough, or that you have already wasted your life. But you are still in His hand. Don't you know that every day with Jesus is a new beginning? The Lord never condemns you or says, "Sorry, you didn't make it." His mercies, He tells us, are new every morning (see Lamentations 3:22–23). Whether you have lost seven days or seventy years, the Lord says to you, "Return to me with all your heart . . . I will repay you for the years the locusts have eaten" (Joel 2:12, 25).

The Lord does not ask you to be a success or a superstar. In fact, if you truly desire to be a revolutionary, here is the second principle: *Give your weaknesses to God so He can use you.* All He requires is a weak, brokenhearted child who will surrender at the foot of the cross.

Look at Gideon's life. The army of the Midianites had invaded Israel and were plundering everything in sight. We are told that "Midian . . . impoverished the Israelites" (Judges 6:6). Gideon was threshing his wheat in a wine-press to hide it from the army when an angel suddenly appeared to him. Did the angel say, "You scared rat, you good-for-nothing runaway"? No, he told Gideon, "The LORD is with you, mighty warrior" (verse 12).

Gideon probably thought, *Who's he talking to? It couldn't be me. Doesn't he see I'm hiding from the Midianites? He must know I'm scared to death.*

But even though that was the way Gideon saw himself, in God he was strong. How? "Not by might nor by power, but by my Spirit" (Zechariah 4:6; see Joel 3:10).

No More Games

The other day I saw a painting that brought tears to my eyes. It was a nighttime scene with a little boy asleep in his bed. He was clutching his teddy bear as he slept peacefully. And there beside the bed was his father, kneeling and praying for him.

As I looked at that picture, I thought of the many times I have knelt beside my son's bed and prayed, "O God, let him live for You."

God is calling all of us to live for Him, to pour ourselves out for others. Become a revolutionary! Here is the third principle: *Live your life with the same heartfelt urgency the father in the picture felt for his son.*

Do you have a family member who does not know Jesus? Begin to pray for him or her. Commit yourself to fast. Pray for your children, your coworkers, your community, for the world. Half the world has never heard the name of Jesus.

Eighty thousand are plunging daily into hell! We must change the course of our generation. And we can do it.

How? A few more dollars?

Money will help, of course. But before you even think about giving more money, your heart must be broken for the lost.

Are you tired of fooling with the world? Living just like everybody else? Do you want to hear the call and be a revolutionary for the Lord?

Come before the presence of the Lord and tell Him you are ready to stop playing games. No more pretend Christianity; you mean business. Commit yourself to living for, not just knowing about, another kingdom—God's Kingdom. Tell Him you are no longer satisfied with knowing all the answers. Now you want to make some serious decisions for your life, starting today, by His grace. This is a new day for you to begin making changes in those areas of your life that you have not yet surrendered to the Lord. And I can assure you, His grace is sufficient.

Stop being satisfied with your own little society. Take the time to learn to pray. Commit your life daily for the sake of His Kingdom. Begin to invest your life in a lost and dying world. If you want to be a world revolutionary, if you want to live for another Kingdom, then your service for the Lord can never be just a few hours of work every day. It must be your life.

Tens of thousands of workers must be sent to the harvest fields, and senders are needed to pray for and support them. Broadcasts need to be aired to the unreached nations. Millions of Bibles need to be distributed. What is missing? People willing to pray, to stand behind those who have gone to the mission field, even to go themselves.

God is not looking for strong, rich, confident people. He is looking for those willing to live according to what they know, committed to a heavenly Kingdom, who come to

Him with their inadequacies and weaknesses, ready to be filled with His power and live with heartfelt urgency to change the world. He is looking for *you*.

That leads us to the ultimate secret that enables us to hear and respond to the call of God.

A Living Sacrifice

The girl was barely fourteen years old when her parents sent her and her older sister to a Christian youth camp for two weeks. There she realized her need for Jesus and committed her life to Him. A few days later she knew the Lord was calling her to serve Him in missions.

When she went home, she devoured the Word of God each day. She spent much time in prayer. Jesus was real to her.

She knew that her parents, who enjoyed a respectable status in the community and many of the good things in life, planned for her and her sister to enter finishing school to learn the cultural graces that would accompany their debut into society. Later they would attend the university and receive the best education available. And eventually they would marry well-to-do men from good families and make their parents proud.

Now, however, this girl's life had changed. Everything she did was based on one question: Does this fall in line with my calling from the Lord? So when the time came for her to enroll in finishing school, she spoke to her parents.

"I belong to Jesus," she told them, "and I've given my life to be a missionary someday. I can't go to this school."

She could tell her parents were confused. And as her relationship with Jesus grew deeper, her life became even more puzzling to them.

"Why are you acting so differently?" they asked. "We can't understand you anymore. Look at your sister—she is acting normally."

Her older sister had a new boyfriend every week, while she had made a decision before the Lord never to date in order to find a husband. Since He knew every hair on her head, He would surely provide a husband for her when she was old enough. She felt no need to go out and "shop around." But she hardly knew how to explain her new devotion.

Meanwhile, she continued to develop her walk with Jesus. She learned to love Him more deeply as time went by. She spent hours in her room, reading her Bible and praying—much of it for missions. By the time she was seventeen or eighteen, she had read more than a hundred books on various cultural groups and missions.

One day she took a small coin from a foreign country and bored a hole into it. Then she put it onto a leather string and tied it around her neck.

Now, she said to herself, *every time I look into the mirror or feel the coin around my neck, it will remind me that I am set apart by the Lord. Twenty-four hours a day I am not my own. I must live to reach the lost.*

The girl chose to go to nursing school, which she felt would give her an advantage on the mission field. As her graduation day neared, her parents and friends approached her.

"Now that you're finally through with your studies," they said, "you should at least take a small vacation and earn a little money before you leave for the mission field, don't you think?"

"I've waited so long to be able to serve the Lord," she responded. "How can I delay any longer?"

The very day she graduated, her bags were packed and she left to join a mission team.

A few years later, while this young woman was serving on the mission field, she met a young, skinny Indian named K. P. Yohannan. She knew this was the man God had chosen for her to marry.

Gisela's willingness to give up her life for Jesus, even at a young age, is what has given her the strength over the years to continue to follow the call of God despite enormous tests and trials.

What Will You Do with Your Self?

This, then, is the ultimate secret: We hear and respond to the call of God when we surrender ourselves to Him. Each of us has been given one life and the choice as to how we will live it. The apostle Paul pleads with us:

I urge you, brothers, in view of God's mercy, to offer your bodies as living sacrifices, holy and pleasing to God— which is your spiritual worship. Do not conform any longer to the pattern of this world, but be transformed by the renewing of your mind. Then you will be able to test and approve what God's will is—his good, pleasing and perfect will.

Romans 12:1–2

There have been many sermons and much exposition on these two verses from Romans. One thing is clear: Whether you were saved last night or fifty years ago, these verses call for absolute surrender of your self to God.

What will you do with your self? E. Stanley Jones addresses some of the choices the world makes in his book *Victory through Surrender*:

Many ancient systems have come to the question of what is to be done with the self and have come to many differing answers. The answers coming out of the East have been, in large measure, answers that show world-weariness. Buddha focused this pervasive disillusionment about the self into the decisive sentence: "Existence and suffering are one." As long as you are in existence you are in suffering. Then the only way to get out of suffering is to get out of desire. . . . So cut the root of desire, become desireless even for life. . . .

Buddha would get rid of the problems of the self by getting rid of self.

Vedantic [Hindu] philosophy says that Brahma is the only reality. But Brahma is the Impersonal. So the devotee sits and in meditation affirms: "Aham Brahma"—I am Brahma. He tries to pass from the personal self to the Impersonal Essence, Brahma. When that transition is made . . . the problems of the self are over.

I asked [a devotee] his name and he replied: "Ram, Ram." I asked him where he had come from and he replied, "Ram, Ram." Where was he going? "Ram, Ram." What did he want? "Ram, Ram." I could get no other reply, for he had vowed to use no name except "Ram, Ram." This was high devotion, but very expensive to the self—it was gone. His face was expressionless. Rama was everything—he was nothing.

When we turn from this world-weariness . . . of the East to modern psychology we find a complete reversal of the attitudes toward the self. Modern psychology has three affirmations about the self: know thy self; accept thy self; express thy self.

What is basically wrong with these three affirmations about the self? Take the first: know thy self. But how can you really know your self by studying your self in relation

to your self, and other human selves, in a purely material
environment? It is all earth-bound, lacks any eternal meaning or goal.

Second: accept thy self. But how can you accept an unac-
ceptable self, a self full of conflicts and contradictions, full
of guilt and frustrations, inferiorities and inhibitions, full
of its self? To ask a man to accept himself—that kind of
self—is to ask the impossible.

Third: secular psychology says: Express thy self. But if
you have a dozen people together all of whom have been
taught to express themselves—what have you got? . . . You
have the stage set for clash and confusion and jealousy and
strife.

What will you do with your self? Many men and women
are still in darkness, trying to figure out the meaning and
purpose of life. But no matter what you try to do with your
self—whether you deny it, obliterate it, annihilate it,
accept it or express it—believe me, it is still alive and
kicking.

Jesus tells us what to do with the self: "If anyone would
come after me, he must deny himself and take up his cross
daily and follow me" (Luke 9:23). But questions remain:
How do we follow Him? *How* do we hear God and implement the power of the Gospel in our lives?

This can happen only through an all-out surrender of
ourselves to the Lord Jesus Christ. It means acknowledg-
ing the Lordship of Christ in our lives, not just in theory
but in practice. Jesus asks us to love Him supremely, more
than anything or anyone else, and to let Him live in us and
through us. Paul expressed it beautifully: "I have been crucified with Christ and I no longer live, but Christ lives in
me" (Galatians 2:20).

When I let Jesus live in and through me, my self is no
longer the one that directs and dictates to me. Now it is
Christ, His will and desires, living and acting through me.

This is why the habit of compartmentalizing our lives must end. All of me, all that I am, belongs to Christ.

It is a daily practice to learn this principle and live it out in our lives. The choices we make are ultimately not collective ones that we make as a church, a family or even a couple. They are choices we make as individuals.

Take a Closer Look

A young missionary lay on her deathbed in India. A friend came up to her and said, "You must feel a little sad to go so early."

"No," she told him with a smile. "Death is mild. My job is finished. I'm going to be with Jesus."

Once your life is given over completely to the Lord, you will no longer be intimidated by circumstances or swayed by what others think. Paul said, "All things are yours, whether Paul or Apollos or Cephas or the world or life or death or the present or the future—all are yours, and you are of Christ, and Christ is of God" (1 Corinthians 3:21–23).

Paul also said, "No matter how many promises God has made, they are 'Yes' in Christ" (2 Corinthians 1:20).

When we understand who Christ is and surrender our lives to Him, we recognize that He is not a tyrant who sits on a high and mighty throne, shaking His finger at us and saying, "No!" Paul tells us that in Jesus all the promises of God are "Yes!"

When the Lord calls you to consecrate your life to Him, He is looking for a living, breathing, moving sacrifice. He wants a total surrender of your will, your intellect, your mind, your five senses, your emotions, your actions.

I pray that you will take a closer look at who you are. From now on you can live your life for a different purpose than for this world alone. I pray that you will hear the call of God and begin to consider eternity as your perspective.

But I must also warn you: If this is your decision, know that you have chosen to walk a narrow road. When Jesus called His disciples to follow Him, He set some conditions before them. The choice you make to follow Christ in-volves a cost. There will be inconveniences, difficulties, pain and counterattack by Satan. (We will look at that counterattack in the next section.)

But praise the Lord, whether you are standing or have fallen, you can rejoice because you have surrendered your self to Him. When everything has been said and done, and the earth as we know it is only a memory, Jesus will say to you, "Well done, good and faithful servant." And His approval is all that matters.

Part 2

OVERCOMING
the OBSTACLES

Only One Concern

Imagine that you have traveled to northern India in the early 1900s to a little village where a tall, turbaned man is the center of attention. A heart-rending scene begins to unfold before you as you watch, invisible to the cast of characters in this real-life drama.

The man, Sadhu Sundar Singh, is about to leave on a long journey. The others, who appear to be his friends, are weeping and begging him not to go. But you can see from Sadhu's face that although he is touched by their love for him, he is determined to go. He says he is on his way back to Tibet, where he has apparently been before—a forbidding land where evil principalities and powers of Buddhism hold the citizens captive. He knows the dangers he faces and so do his friends and coworkers.

They continue to cry out, "Please don't leave us!"

But Sadhu tells them, "I must go."

The curtain falls on this scene and rises on another one. Sadhu has arrived in Tibet and is preaching the Gospel openly, but he has been seized by the *lamas,* the

Buddhist priests. He threatens their existence and they act accordingly.

They fling Sadhu Sundar Singh into the death well, a place no one has ever escaped. A bone in his arm crunches painfully beneath him as he lands. He hears the key turning in the cover of the well. His eyes grow accustomed to the murky darkness. Snakes writhe in the dank hole. Rats skitter around him. He can feel around him the skulls and bones of those who have been thrown into the well before him.

As Sadhu lies there with a broken arm in the midst of the filth, he begins to pray: "Lord, I am so grateful that You have given me this privilege to suffer for Your name's sake."

Over and over he repeats this prayer as the night grows deeper and darker.

Suddenly the well cover opens and a rope is thrown down. After a few seconds of amazement, Sadhu grasps for the rope and is pulled out of his filthy tomb. When he reaches the top of the well, no one is there.

In the next scene we see Sadhu preaching once again in the streets of the Tibetan village. The lamas are confounded, for they know that only the head lama has the key to the death well.

Let's allow the curtain to fall on the drama and take a closer look at the life of this early twentieth-century missionary. We know from books and oral accounts that Sadhu Sundar Singh underwent times of intense persecution and hardship. Ultimately he laid down his life in Tibet for the sake of the Gospel.

Yet as this real event from his life shows, something allowed him to rise above his circumstances—something that enabled him to endure and even rejoice in hardship because he considered it a privilege to serve and suffer.

Sadhu Sundar Singh had the key to what many of us are looking for.

Horizontal Motivation

As human beings we cannot survive any commitment for long without motivation, whether it is godly or self-centered.

Self-centered motivation can be money, power, appreciation—anything that gratifies us. Have you ever wondered why some people tolerate boredom, frustration or pain just to work at a job they hate intensely? They dislike everyone there and cannot stand what they do, but they stay with it anyway. Why? Because they get a paycheck every week. That is their motivation.

Self-centered motivation has its spiritual side, too. We may do wonderful things for the Kingdom because we want to look good, or because we feel guilty if we do not do this or that, or because we got charged emotionally from some challenge we heard in the pulpit. It is easy to fall into the trap of horizontal motivation. Our motives may be impure but, we think to ourselves, *Who knows? And does it really matter?*

It *does* matter when we convey the outward appearance of holiness without the inward foundation. Here is what A. W. Tozer said about horizontal motivation in his book *The Root of the Righteous:*

The test by which all conduct must finally be judged is motive.

As water cannot rise higher than its source, so the moral quality in an act can never be higher than the motive that inspires it. For this reason no act that arises from an evil motive can be good, even though some good may appear to come out of it. Every deed done out of anger or spite, for instance, will be found at last to have been done for the enemy and against the Kingdom of God.

Unfortunately, the nature of religious activity is such that much of it can be carried on for reasons that are not good, such as anger, jealousy, ambition, vanity and avarice.

All such activity is essentially evil, and will be counted as such at the judgment.

In this matter of motive, as in so many other things, the Pharisees afford us clear examples. They remain the world's most dismal religious failures, not because of doctrinal error nor because they were careless or lukewarm, nor because they were outwardly persons of dissolute life. Their whole trouble lay in the quality of their religious motives. They prayed, but they prayed to be heard of men, and thus their motives ruined their prayers and rendered them not only useless, but actually evil. They gave generously to the service of the temple, but they sometimes did it to escape their duty toward their parents, and this was an evil. They judged sin and stood against it when they found it in others, but this they did from self-righteousness and hardness of their heart.

So with almost everything they did. Their activities had about them an outward appearance of holiness, and those same activities, if carried on out of pure motives, would have been good and praiseworthy. The whole weakness of the Pharisees lay in the quality of their motives.

That this is not a small matter may be gathered from the fact that those orthodox and proper religionists went on in their blindness till they at last crucified the Lord of glory with no inkling of the gravity of their crime.

Horizontal motivation will not sustain us long. It takes only a few people, a few challenging circumstances or an unfavorable environment to cause us to fizzle out in our activity for the Kingdom. From the inside we can muster up only so much strength.

We need continuous input. The physical life, in which we must have food and water to survive, illustrates what is needed in the inner man as well. We need motivation that is objective—from the Lord.

Vertical Motivation

The life of the apostle Paul is the story of any "normal" Christian. Paul was no superstar or extra-anointed person. He crafted tents with his hands, making his living like anyone else. But every tent he made, every trip he made to the market, every voyage he took in a ship, was incidental to his real goal in life: to pull a few more people out of the fires of hell.

About reaching his own people, Paul wrote, "For I could wish that I myself were cursed and cut off from Christ for the sake of my brothers, those of my own race, the people of Israel" (Romans 9:3–4). Paul was ready to give his life if it meant the Jews would be saved. Why? And what kept him going when he was misunderstood and forsaken by those around him? When he was left to die after being stoned? When he was shipwrecked?

Paul tells us in 2 Corinthians 5:14 that "Christ's love compels us." The Amplified Version uses the words *controls and urges and impels*. Paul was not moved to live as he lived by any factor other than his relationship with the Lord. He was motivated to do everything he did for one reason: Jesus.

God said regarding Paul when he was first converted, "I will show him how much he must suffer for my name" (Acts 9:16). Later Paul himself, in his letter to the Philippians, wrote, "For to me, to live is Christ and to die is gain" (Philippians 1:21). Paul could live like this and endure hardships because of one thing: *He lived constantly for the approval of his Master.*

Hebrews 12:3 admonishes us to "consider him who endured such opposition from sinful men, so that you will not grow weary and lose heart."

Psalm 119 contains two dynamic verses that deal with this vertical, objective motivation from the Lord.

First the psalmist wrote, "Indignation grips me" (verse 53).

Have you ever seen how a ravenous lion holds his helpless prey by the scruff of the neck? That is how the psalmist felt—that "burning indignation" (NASB) had grabbed hold of him. Had someone beaten him up? Had someone violated his rights? Had he lost his salary or had to keep working overtime? No, he was indignant "because of the wicked, who have forsaken your law."

Now verse 136: "Streams of tears flow from my eyes."

In our culture people experience all kinds of hurt, whether through personal problems or situations imposed on us. Our own sins may hurt us, our expectations may not be met, other people may fail us or harsh circumstances may bear down on us. There are many reasons we experience sorrow, pain, agony, self-pity, discouragement, disillusionment, mental breakdown, even suicide.

I remember when my mother died. *If I don't control myself*, I thought when my mother's body was carried from our house to the cemetery, *I know I will begin to cry. I need to be rational about this. I know she is happy with the Lord and in the best place she can be. I'll see her soon.* But when I saw others weeping out loud, I completely lost it. I sobbed. As I walked outside, following the casket, I could not even stand up; I had to hold onto a tree for support.

But my weeping lasted a few hours, perhaps a day at the most. This man was brokenhearted and could not stop crying. Why? Because "your law is not obeyed."

All his grief had to do with one small word: *Your.*

You Are Mine, Life Is Yours

One of the most beautiful statements I have ever read on genuine vertical motivation was made by E. Stanley Jones in his book *Victory through Surrender*. He made it a habit to spend time before the Lord during "a time in the

early morning when I don't ask for anything but listen to
see if God has anything to say to me." This is what Jones
heard one day:

> He said to me, "You are Mine, life is yours." I was startled
> and asked Him to repeat it. And He did: "You are Mine,
> life is yours."
>
> That saying has been singing its way through my heart
> ever since: If I belong to Christ, life belongs to me; I can
> master it, rescue some good out of everything, good, bad
> and indifferent. . . . I do not have to be concerned about
> this, that or the other. I have one concern and only one—
> that I be His.

If you want to stand firm when trials come, like Sadhu
Sundar Singh; not be moved by circumstances; not waver
in your faith—then know that you cannot even begin to
do it in your own strength. For the people of God to stand
firm and even to survive in the days to come, we must relinquish our lives and all they mean to Jesus.

Your only concern is to be His—to be approved by Him,
to please Him, to belong to Him. All that you are and do
must be centered around Him and His purposes. Then, as
you walk through life, every emotion you feel and every
circumstance you face will be secondary. Are you His? Then
life is yours.

In the next chapter we will take a closer look at motivation—signs that we are horizontally motivated and steps
to make us more vertically motivated.

What Motivates You?

The man stopped hoeing and straightened up, wiping sweat and grime from his forehead. He thought he had heard unusual sounds coming from the house. Strains of music drifted across the field and, he thought, shouts and laughter as well. What was going on?

Well, it was 'way past quitting time anyway. He swung the hoe over his shoulder and trudged over the freshly turned-up field toward the house.

As he drew nearer, the music grew louder. He could tell the wine must be flowing freely; the dancing and merriment were in full swing.

Father must have real reason for celebration, he thought.

Just then a servant came scurrying out.

"What's going on?" he asked.

"Your brother has come home!" the servant replied. "Your father has killed the fatted calf, and we are all rejoicing because your brother is safe and sound. Please, your father wants you to join the celebration—come!"

The man's face darkened. So this was what they were celebrating—his brother's return? His irresponsible, wild, loose-living, inheritance-wasting brother? How dare he return after all the years of grief and uncertainty he had caused! A storehouse of angry memories flooded him.

"I will have no part of this celebration!" he spat at the servant. "You can tell my father I will not go in!"

And he turned on his heel.

We are all familiar with the story in Luke 15 of the man and his two sons. We know the younger brother as the Prodigal Son, but the story is really about the love of his father.

Jesus had been criticized by the Pharisees and scribes because He chose to eat with the publicans and sinners. "Look at this man," they whispered to each other. "He says He's God, but look who He eats with!"

Jesus' dinner companions were indeed reputed to be the worst members of society. But the Pharisees misunderstood God's holiness to mean He would have nothing to do with sinners. So Jesus told them the story of the man and his sons to show them the heart of the Father. He was saying to them, "God has *everything* to do with sinners, because He loves them."

Jolting the Jar

It is plain to see that the younger son represents the sinner, the outcast. But let's take a closer look at the older son.

The older son is a picture of the believer, someone who knows the Lord and is within the fold of believers. What was he doing when the younger son finally returned? Working out in the fields. He was committed to his father and to his work. In appearance, anyhow, he loved his father more than his brother did. He never left home or gambled his money away.

The older brother is a classic illustration of the individual who seems to be doing a lot of good and whose life is full of activity but who may be motivated horizontally, not vertically. The motivation keeping the older brother going was not genuine love for his father. When his brother returned and adverse circumstances bore down on him, the truth came out.

Someone once said, "If you fill a jar with honey and jolt it as hard as you can, no bitter water will ever come out."

The older brother was "perfect." He sacrificed and worked long hours. He gave money faithfully for missions every month. He cut back on his lifestyle and lived more simply. He prayed an hour every day. He was active in his church. He always went the extra mile.

Am I talking about you and me? I am. But as we are in the midst of good activity, sometimes things begin to go wrong. *Wow!* we say to ourselves. *I didn't realize I would ever face rejection for doing the right thing. I thought everyone would appreciate my hard work. I thought I'd get a few rewards, a little recognition. . . .*

When external pressures bear upon us and jolt the jar, whatever is inside comes out. This jolting is orchestrated by the Lord, who wants us to see what is really in our hearts.

Why did the older son act the way he did? He felt taken for granted, and was angry with his father for receiving his younger brother back, who had done wrong while he had done right.

If we look carefully at Luke 15, we can see at least nine signs that something was missing in the older brother. He had lost the genuine motivation of his heart—his love for his father.

Let's look at each of these signs.

Legalism

Strangely enough, the person who has lost authentic vertical motivation from the Lord falls into *legalism*. The love of Christ no longer constrains him. He works for the sake of the work alone, whereas true motivation in working for the Kingdom of God is love.

Love is the oil that keeps the machinery running smoothly. With this motivation there is no murmuring, no complaining, no grouchiness. People motivated by the love of God can serve Him 24 hours a day and be the happiest people in the world. They cannot do enough for the Lord because they love Him so much. When you lose that vertical motivation, you are doing things for the Lord because you *have* to.

Legalism also means serving only for the reward. The older brother tells his father, "Look! All these years I've been slaving for you . . . yet you never gave me even a young goat so I could celebrate with my friends" (verse 29).

When a person loses the love motive of his heart, he sees the Father as mean and unfair. He begins to compare service records. The older brother compared his work with that of his younger brother, who wasted and destroyed everything his father had given him.

The man in Jesus' parable of the talents who buried the one talent he had been given told his master, "I knew that you are a hard man" (Matthew 25:24). He saw his master as unloving and cruel.

Then there is the parable of the vineyard owner who gave equal wages to all his workers, whether they began at nine in the morning or four in the afternoon. The ones who had started work early began to grumble.

"These men who were hired last worked only one hour," they said, "and you have made them equal to us who have borne the burden of the work and the heat of the day."

But he answered one of them, "Friend, I am not being unfair to you. Didn't you agree to work for a denarius? Take your pay and go."

Matthew 20:12–14

I like the story in Genesis 29 about Jacob. Good old Jacob—what a rude awakening to find out that the woman you married was not the one you meant to marry! Yet we read that all those years of hard labor for Rachel "seemed like only a few days to him *because of his love for her*" (verse 20, italics added). He was not working just to feed a few sheep. He was not working for pay. The focus of all his labors was Rachel alone.

I spoke to a group of people once who were working with a Christian organization on the mission field, and I asked them to think about this question: "If your entire allowance were gone, if your benefits disappeared, if next month you would not earn even a penny—would you still come here? If you had no money even to ride a bus to the office, would you walk here and serve the Lord anyway?"

This is the kind of question we must ask ourselves if we want to avoid the trap of legalism.

Self-Pity, Bitterness, Discouragement

The father, weeping and rejoicing over his younger son, pleaded with his elder son to come in. But the son refused. His unyielding, headstrong disposition is a clear indication that he was not motivated by love for his father. He refused to go in because he felt sorry for himself. He was bitter about his situation. And he was discouraged.

But *self-pity, bitterness and discouragement* have nothing to do with genuine vertical motivation.

The older brother had little feeling for his father or brother. His feelings had festered so long that he could think only about himself.

Jealousy and Love for Honor or Position

Third, a person not motivated by love for the Lord will experience *jealousy* over others' blessings and the *desire for honor and position*. He may want to be noticed by others, looking for opportunities to tell them what he has done. He may be dissatisfied with second place. Or he may secretly expect appreciation or approval. When our hearts are not motivated by love, our relationships with others are strained.

The older brother had apparently been content working in the fields day after day. But when his brother came home, he became jealous.

Now that this brother of mine has returned, he thought, *look at the hugs, the ring, the shoes, the new clothes. Look at the feast, the dancing, the celebration. All the attention I've gotten, all the benefits I've received, all my father's love, will now be turned to him.*

Take another New Testament example. Before Paul's conversion on the Damascus road, he wanted to eliminate Christianity. If you had been a believer during that time, you would have had a hard time accepting this new convert.

"It's just a ploy," you might have said. "He's only coming to find out who we are. Then he'll kill us."

This is exactly what those believers thought. No one trusted Paul(see Acts 9:26). Then Barnabas came along and put his life on the line. He vouched for Paul and convinced others that Paul had truly been saved. A wonderful partnership was begun. But a few chapters later in Acts, we no longer read about "Barnabas and Paul." Now we read about "Paul and Barnabas." Fascinating! Barnabas took second place to Paul because his motivation was not based on honor or position. Barnabas simply loved Jesus and wanted to serve Him.

It is a sign of true godliness to desire nothing but the Lord Himself. It is no simple thing to take second place and let someone else get the honor. It can be done only by someone who loves God.

Pride

The older brother told his father, "All these years I have done your work," revealing an "I'm-better-than-my-brother" attitude. He also complained about "this son of yours" (verse 30). Notice that he did not say "my brother" but "your son."

He was filled with *pride*, an exalted opinion of himself. Pride is the fourth indication that a believer is not motivated by love for God. The older brother did not even have room in his heart to acknowledge the tramp weeping and repenting as his brother. There was no room in his life for weak people. In his eyes he was plainly superior.

When we work as a team, as a church, as a fellowship, we must remember that the Body of Christ is made up not of superhuman entities but of weak, broken-legged, half-blind, bruised, hurting, sinning and repenting people. And it seems to me from this story that God has more compassion for them than for the "superstars."

This story is about the all-embracing, all-forgiving, all-encompassing love of a father. But his older son, who lived in the same house and worked for him, was untouched by his love and made no concession for the weak, failed, backslidden man who stood before him. All he could say was, "He had it coming."

True motivation from the Lord, by contrast, manifests itself in humility.

Lack of Love for Others

We do not read that the older son went out to look for his brother when he was gone. And who had told him his brother was living with prostitutes and doing wicked things? Not his brother! Still, the older son told his father: "This son of yours . . . has squandered your property with prostitutes. . ." (Luke 15:30). There was *no love* in his heart; he expected the worst from his brother.

Jonah had no love in his heart, either. He preached a fiery sermon, warning the Ninevites that they would soon be destroyed for their wickedness. But when the city repented and God decided not to destroy them, Jonah was angry with God:

> "O LORD, is this not what I said when I was still at home? That is why I was so quick to flee to Tarshish. I knew that you are a gracious and compassionate God, slow to anger and abounding in love, a God who relents from sending calamity."
>
> Jonah 4:2

What a strange rationalization! Jonah knew his theology but it was only head knowledge. He anticipated God's compassion but did not understand or share it. He was not motivated by love.

Then there was Ruth. In the first chapter of that fantastic drama, Naomi tells her daughters-in-law, Ruth and Orpah, "Look, my children, this is it. There's nothing I can do for you. Your husbands are both dead and I have no more sons for you to marry. Go home and find new husbands."

> Then Orpah kissed her mother-in-law good-by, but Ruth clung to her. . . . "Don't urge me to leave you or to turn back from you. Where you go I will go, and where you stay I will stay. Your people will be my people and your God my God."
>
> Ruth 1:14, 16

Going with Naomi meant that Ruth would be leaving behind all that was familiar—her family, her culture, even the gods she worshiped. How could Ruth make such a decision? Because she loved Naomi. *Love made it possible for her to leave everything.*

When you lack love for your brothers and sisters around you, becoming short-tempered and impatient and expecting the worst from others, it indicates you are not motivated by the love of the Father.

Wanting to Give Up

The sixth sign of erosion in genuine motivation is *desiring simply to quit.* The older son refused to go inside and join the celebration. He was saying to his father, "I've done all these things for you and what have you done for me? I'm the one who has to give and give and give. Seems like a one-way street to me. I'm getting the short end of the stick."

Everyone at some point faces the temptation to quit. Some are tempted to give up their Christian life entirely. In 2 Timothy 4:10 Paul told Timothy that Demas had packed up his bags and left him.

If anyone ever had a reason to quit, Paul did. But he was motivated by something beyond what he could see. "I can do everything through him who gives me strength," he said (Philippians 4:13).

Unwillingness to Suffer

Inconveniences, trials, difficulties and living with less cause many people to lose their motivation. This is the seventh indicator of a lack of authentic vertical motivation: *refusal to accept suffering as part of love.*

The elder son lacked something his father had—a tender heart toward his brother. Any feelings of love he might ever have had were buried deep beneath his resentment, bitterness and anger. But his father was not afraid to love his youngest son, even if it meant suffering terrible hurt over the poor choices his son had made.

No love is genuine unless it includes suffering. C. S. Lewis wrote about the risks of true love in his book *The Four Loves*:

> To love at all is to be vulnerable. Love anything, and your heart will certainly be wrung and possibly be broken. If you want to make sure of keeping it intact, you must give your heart to no one, not even to an animal. Wrap it carefully round with hobbies and little luxuries; avoid all entangle-ments; lock it up safe in the casket or coffin of your self-ishness. But in that casket—safe, dark, motionless, air-less—it will change. It will not be broken; it will become unbreakable, impenetrable, irredeemable.
>
> The alternative to tragedy, or at least to the risk of tragedy, is damnation. The only place outside Heaven where you can be perfectly safe from all the dangers and perturbations of love is Hell.

Jesus' motivation was pure love for His Father. In obe-dience He came as a man and shared His Father's heart for the lost world. And the love that was in His heart included suffering. If it had not, we would not have a Redeemer.

Lack of Prayer

Although it is not specifically mentioned in the story, I seriously doubt that the older son had any real heart-to-heart communication with his father. And this is the eighth sign that genuine vertical motivation is lacking: *a lack of prayer*.

Any church or organization not motivated by love for God will rely on agencies, plans, programs, schedules and all sorts of gimmicks to get the job done. If we are not motivated to do what we do by the love of God, we will surely dry up in our prayer lives, too.

What keeps us going in feast and famine is the kind of relationship with the Lord that only prayer can bring.

Unwillingness to Live by Faith

The father told his older son, "You are always with me, and everything I have is yours" (Luke 15:31). He was saying, "All that you see around you—look! It's yours! It's always been yours, whether now or later. I love you, and I care about your younger brother, too. It's all the same."

But the son could not understand what his father was telling him. And this is the final sign: *unwillingness to live by faith.*

Paul told Timothy, "The time has come for my departure. . . . Now there is in store for me the crown of righteousness, which the Lord, the righteous Judge, will award to me on that day" (2 Timothy 4:6, 8). Paul looked forward to that day in faith.

We read in Hebrews 11 of a group of people who lived, suffered and died in faith. Even though they did not experience the promises of the Lord in their generation, they looked toward the day when those promises would be fulfilled.

When you do not look to Him as your source, your circumstances can look pretty grim. And when your faith in the Lord runs short, you know you are not being motivated by love for Him.

Regaining Our Motivation

Have you lost the vital vertical motivation of love for God? Have you caught glimpses of yourself in the pages you have just read?

Horizontally motivated persons can be involved vigorously in the work of the Lord. They can also be demanding and judgmental. They may express intense concern about the moral condition of society or become zealous for world evangelism. But when the internal relationship is gone, only a shadow of that reality remains.

Paul talked about a group of people who were sold out to preaching the Gospel, but for the wrong motivation. They intended to cause more persecution for Paul, who was in prison at the time for preaching the Gospel (see Philippians 1:15–17).

In 2 Samuel 12, when Nathan approached David after his sin with Bathsheba, Nathan told him a story about two men. One was a rich, greedy man who owned many sheep; the other was a poor man who owned only one little lamb. When he told David that the rich man had taken the only lamb of his poor neighbor and slaughtered it to feed a visitor, David was enraged.

"Who is the rat?" he thundered to Nathan. "He deserves to die!"

Then Nathan told David, "You are the man."

David had been so zealous for his people and so out of touch with God that he failed to see he was the real culprit.

It is easy to get out of touch with God and try to live the Christian life on our own. We all fall into it. But when we realize what has gone wrong, how do we go about mending it?

Repent

In Revelation we read Jesus' message to the church in Ephesus—an incredible passage that can turn your stomach inside-out! If you remember the story of the Ephesians from Acts 19, you know that when Paul preached the Gospel to them, a great number believed. They brought their sorcery books, worth 50,000 pieces of silver, and burned them publicly. They took a stand against darkness and committed themselves to Christ, separating themselves from their former ways of living.

Paul wrote that the Ephesians were blessed with "every spiritual blessing" (Ephesians 1:3) and prayed for them for "the Spirit of wisdom and revelation" (verse 17). But now Jesus told them:

> "I know your deeds, your hard work and your perseverance. I know that you cannot tolerate wicked men, that you have tested those who claim to be apostles but are not, and have found them false. You have persevered and have endured hardships for my name, and have not grown weary.
>
> "Yet I hold this against you: You have forsaken your first love. Remember the height from which you have fallen! Repent and do the things you did at first. If you do not repent, I will come to you and remove your lampstand from its place."
>
> Revelation 2:2–5

There is a fascinating paradox in this passage. First Jesus is positive: "You are doing many good things." Then He says, "Repent and do the same things."

Perhaps the Lord would say something similar to a believer today: "You are giving ten thousand dollars every month to My work, but I am going to snuff out your light unless you repent."

"Lord," says the believer, "what do You want me to do?"

"Repent; then give ten thousand dollars a month to My work."

At first it sounds confusing, doesn't it? But Jesus was saying something was missing in the Ephesians' lives. They were laboring the same as always, but their inner motivation had changed. It was no longer "labor prompted by love" (1 Thessalonians 1:3). They had forsaken their first love.

When you find yourself in a situation like this, the Lord wants you to come to Him and say something like this:

"Lord, I'm still doing all these things, but now it's only mechanical. The spring is wound and things keep going, but my heart for You is no longer involved. I don't have the same love for the lost; I do these things because I have to do them. It's been a long time, Lord, since I cried over the lost world. My concerns have turned to myself and my own problems. Please, Lord, give me that genuine heart motivation once again."

This is true repentance—not patching up old wineskins, but becoming new wineskins altogether. I encourage you to take this first step of repentance.

Surrender

I thank God for the day more than twenty years ago when a group of Operation Mobilization workers, including me, gathered in an old school building in North India. George Verwer spoke to us from Hebrews 4 with this message: "There remains a rest for God's people. Enter into it."

I will never forget that day. It was the day I surrendered myself completely to the Lord. I was one of the ones who went forward and said, "I'm fighting, struggling and striving. I'm always hurting and in pain. I'm always complaining that something is wrong. I want rest."

That day I began to realize the incredible reality of entering God's rest. Once you surrender your life completely to the Lord, no matter what happens from then on, you have something to fall back on. It is all in God's hands.

Be Filled with the Holy Spirit

There is no more important factor in living a victorious life—one filled with motivation and strength that come from beyond ourselves—than being filled with the Holy

Spirit. But many are confused about what it means to be filled with the Holy Spirit.

I will not dictate to you about *how* to be filled with the Spirit of God. It does not matter to me how it happens; just make sure that you *are!*

The Word of God tells us we are walking into dangerous times in history when many will fall away. We must not be persuaded by the trends of this world. Remember, God wiped out a whole generation and saved only Noah and his family. The majority of *this* generation will not make it. But a minority are living holy lives, led by the Spirit of God, willing to walk in Jesus' footsteps and trying to reach others for Him.

As unto the Lord

What is the key to living with right motivation? Do everything "as to the Lord, and not unto men" (Colossians 3:23, KJV). Even though we hear this statement often, the real meaning comes when we interpret it practically.

It is said that if we do anything for 21 days, we will have established a habit. Let me suggest, then, that for the next 21 days, no matter what you are asked to do, you say to yourself, "I am doing it for the Lord. I am doing it for the Lord."

Watch how this becomes part of your thinking—and part of your life!

Think about Heaven

Why should we think about heaven? Because it is the "paycheck" Paul said he was looking for when he wrote, "There is in store for me the crown of righteousness" (2 Timothy 4:8).

Heaven is not our motivation, as the older brother was motivated by the thought of his reward and not by love for his father. But we will find joy in thinking about heaven as we serve our heavenly Father in love.

Isaiah prophesied, "See, the Sovereign LORD comes with power. . . . See, his reward is with him" (Isaiah 40:10).

Daniel was pulled out of his homeland, put into prison, given a job, then misunderstood. He had no wife or children. His life was one of giving and serving, giving and serving. He was thrown into the lions' den but kept on serving. Kings came and went and the kingdom of Babylon changed hands. Daniel had to prove himself again and again.

At the very end of the book, when Daniel had become an old man, an angel appeared to him and told him, "Go your way till the end. You will rest, and then at the end of the days you will rise to receive your allotted inheritance" (Daniel 12:13).

Why, in the last part of this faithful old man's life, did God send His angel to tell him these words? I do not know, but I suspect that Daniel, in all the ups and downs of his life and after all his troubling visions of the end times, had something on his mind.

Someday, he may have thought to himself, *this is all going to be over. This is not final. This is just a short time that I have to walk through.*

So when the angel spoke to him, it affirmed his convictions.

And Paul, in the final stage of his life, told Timothy he knew there was a crown reserved for him. That knowledge kept him going so that he could say confidently, "Our light and momentary troubles are achieving for us an eternal glory that far outweighs them all" (2 Corinthians 4:17).

Think about heaven. In everything you have to deal with each day, think, *This is not the end. There is much more. This is only a short time that I am walking through.* The Lord has promised us through His Word that the end will be far better than the beginning. Do not lose heart. Take Him at His Word!

Bringing
Our Hearts
Back into Focus

I plopped down in an empty chair in the terminal at Chicago's O'Hare International Airport and heaved a big sigh. I had sixteen days of nonstop traveling and speaking behind me and now had two hours between plane connections to catch my breath. Usually I do not mind waiting awhile in the terminal—I enjoy watching people—but on this day I was tired of it.

Why am I doing this? I asked myself. *What's it all about, anyway?*

I was exhausted from sleeping in strange hotel beds with pillows that seemed to grow harder every night. Even the hot chili powder I brought with me to spice up my food had run out. After pouring my heart out to groups all over the country, I was drained and angry with the world. I was even angry with my office staff for booking all these speaking engagements. I had approved the meetings, of course, but it felt better to shift the blame away from myself.

I walked over to a pay phone and dialed the Gospel for Asia office in Dallas. I do not even recall who answered the phone.

"This is K. P.," I said tersely. "I just want to say one thing: Do not book any meetings ever again unless you check with me directly first."

When I hung up, I felt worse than ever.

"Don't these people understand I'm not a machine?" I said to myself aloud. "I'm only a human being."

As I wallowed in my self-pity, I knew I had to get up and go on, no matter how I felt. And there was a plane to catch. But how was I to find the strength to continue?

None of us remains the same in our enthusiasm and commitment. If we do not feed continually on the things of the Lord—His Word and His presence—we cannot hope to finish the race.

You may have begun your walk with the Lord with wholehearted enthusiasm, ready to die for the cause of the lost world. As followers of Jesus, after all, our purpose in life is not to build an organization, attain financial security, be loved or respected or remembered for noble deeds. What really matters is what Jesus said in the Great Commission: Focusing our hearts on reaching this generation with the Gospel.

But as time went by, certain things began to eat at that purpose—the distractions and cares of the world, your own personal problems, discouragement, fears, the enticements of your friends. Suddenly you find yourself looking for a way to get out of the battle. Maybe your Christian life is just not challenging enough. Maybe it no longer seems worth investing your life in. Maybe when you first made your commitment, the leaders in your church or Bible study were on fire for the Lord and really helped you grow, but now that you have known them longer, you see areas of compromise.

Shifting the blame, just as I did at the airport, is an easy way out. I have seen this happen in many organizations and many lives. What is actually happening here? Over a period of time we can lose our focus.

God told the children of Israel,

> Remember how the LORD your God led you all the way in the desert these forty years, to humble you and to test you in order to know what was in your heart, whether or not you would keep his commands.
>
> Deuteronomy 8:2

God allows adverse circumstances for a reason—whether they be weaknesses, people we work with who rub us the wrong way, decisions we must make that go against our emotions, unfulfilled expectations, misunderstandings, ingratitude, loss of our rights, shattered hopes. Suddenly in the midst of our labors for His Kingdom, God takes us and says, "You are in the wilderness. I want to see what will keep you going. When your emotions run dry, when your feelings are gone and there is nothing left to hold onto but bare facts—will you stay with Me?"

Out of the Shadow-Lands

As I wallowed in the muck of my self-pity at O'Hare Airport that day, I had one of those rare encounters with the Lord. Right there at the gate, it was as if time stopped for a few moments.

I heard a voice in my heart asking me, *Who asked you to do all these things? Didn't I tell you that My yoke is easy and My burden is light? Who made it so hard?*

Spiritually, I realized, I was dry inside. I had been so busy in my service for the Lord that I had lost sight of the Lord whom I was serving. I no longer had the continual out-pouring of Christ's strength that Paul talked about: "I can do everything through him who gives me strength" (Philippians 4:13).

Lord, I said, *I know what You are telling me is true. I am so depressed and tired and weak. But Lord, I want You to help me.*

At this point the ticket counter had opened for passengers to check in and get their boarding passes. I could see the gate behind it just beginning to open. Soon I would walk through that doorway and board the plane. Suddenly, as I looked at it, the Lord painted a wonderful picture before my mind's eye.

A few weeks earlier I had finished reading *The Last Battle,* the final book in C. S. Lewis' classic allegorical series *The Chronicles of Narnia.* In them Lewis tells the story of the adventures of eight English children in the land of Narnia with Aslan, the great lion, who portrays a type of Christ. *The Last Battle* recounts the end of the age for Narnia. As the children watch through a doorway, the old world is destroyed before their eyes and another land opens up before them.

It seems to them almost exactly like the old, yet different, somehow. Digory, one of the older children, explains it to the rest:

"... The Narnia you were thinking of ... was not the real Narnia. That had a beginning and an end. It was only a shadow or a copy of the real Narnia, which has always been here and always will be here. ... You need not mourn over Narnia. ... All of the old Narnia that mattered, all the dear creatures, have been drawn into the real Narnia through the Door. And of course it is different; as different as a real thing is from a shadow or as waking life is from a dream."

Lewis concludes the book (and the series) this way:

And for us this is the end of all the stories, and we can most
truly say that they all lived happily ever after. But for them
it was only the beginning of the real story. All their life in
this world and all their adventures in Narnia had only been
the cover and title page: now at last they were beginning
Chapter One of the Great Story, which no one on earth
has read: which goes on forever: in which every chapter is
better than the one before.

As I recalled these final scenes from the book, it was time
for me to board my plane.

Then the fog of my self-pity vanished. I could see clearly
once again. I realized that all my aches and pains, my schedule, the bland food, the hard pillows, the strange beds—all
these were just a shadow of what was yet to come. My everyday life here on earth was not the real thing. It was tem-
porary and would soon pass.

I looked toward the gate and thought about the door
the children had gone through to leave "the Shadow-
Lands," as Lewis called them, and enter "the real Narnia." It was time for me to live again, not for the illusion,
but for the reality. That gate to my flight was a door to
that reality, if I would choose to accept what was set before
me.

I jumped to my feet. I knew I had the strength of the
Lord to face the tasks before me. Nothing could stop me
now! I marched straight for that boarding gate, through
the threshold and onto my next connection. The attitude
of my heart was changed. I was no longer running on empty.
Once again the strength I was receiving was not my own;
it was from the Lord.

And the meetings that followed were different somehow. I could tell that, despite the inconveniences, the
tiredness and the discomfort, my heart was in focus once
again.

The Bottom Line

Within the past decade the world has experienced events that no one dreamed about. We have stood by in amazement while whole countries were reshaped practically overnight, world systems crumbled into the pages of history books and political maps changed faster than cartographers could redraw them. For all this to happen, there must have been a tremendous confrontation of spiritual forces in the unseen world. We can see the effects of it on the cutting edge of missions. The hand of God is moving in an unprecedented way. People are hungry for the living God in a way that we did not see even ten or twenty years ago.

We may not understand all that is taking place in the spiritual realm, but this one thing is clear: The coming of Jesus Christ is very near. Right now the possibility to reach our generation with the Gospel is better than at any other time in history. The opportunities are unlimited and the Church has the resources.

But what I see happening in Christian circles concerns me deeply. Believers are being bombarded from all sides to invest their time, efforts and finances in everything but a lost and dying world. Material things, trips, social gatherings, building projects, the comfort of their families—all these and more may come at the expense of souls who are lost for eternity. And believers who have already committed their lives to reaching the world with the Gospel are in danger of losing their focus. When emotions are down and times are difficult, it is easy to focus on self and want out of the battle.

Ultimately two major forces influence what happens on earth: the living God and the powers of darkness—Satan and his demons. The Lord, through His mercy, is seeking to bring as many people as possible to repentance, so they might know Him and reign with Him forever. Satan, on the other hand, is seeking to take as many people as possible with him into hell.

One of the most successful ways he does this is by causing us believers to forget our purpose. He wants to get us so wrapped up in who we are and what we are doing day to day that we are no longer able to answer the questions *Why am I here?* and *What am I living for?*

Why *are* we here on earth? What is the purpose behind our lives? It is for the multiplied millions of people, more than two billion of them, in fact, who have not yet been reached with the Gospel and are on their way to hell. They are not rats or snakes or monkeys, but human beings like you and me, and just as precious in the sight of God.

If you were inside your home and suddenly heard someone outside yelling, "Your house is on fire—get out, get out!" would you stand there and talk it over with your family? Of course not! You would find any way possible to get out.

The situation in the world is much worse than a house on fire. The souls of more than two billion people are at stake and we have an opportunity to take countless ones with us to heaven instead of allowing them to die in their sins. So how can we live comfortably for ourselves while millions slip into an eternal hell?

We can do it because the enemy has managed to replace our focus on eternity with a focus on other things. Gayle Erwin, one of the board members for Gospel for Asia and a very dear friend, shared with me a modern-day parable that sheds light on the condition of the Church today:

> On a dangerous seacoast where shipwrecks often occurred, there was once a crude little lifesaving station. The building was just a hut, and there was only one boat; but the few devoted members kept a constant watch over the sea. And with no thought for themselves, they went out day and night, tirelessly searching for the lost.

Some of those who were saved and various others in the surrounding area wanted to become associated with the station and give of their time and money and effort for the support of its work. New boats were bought, and new crews were trained. The little lifesaving station grew.

Some of the members of the lifesaving station were unhappy that the building was so crude and poorly equipped. They felt that a more comfortable place should be provided as the first refuge for those saved from the sea. They replaced the emergency cots with beds and put better furniture in the enlarged building.

The lifesaving station became a popular gathering place for its members, and they decorated it beautifully and furnished it exquisitely, because they used it as a sort of club. Fewer members were now interested in going out to sea on lifesaving missions, so they hired lifeboat crews to do the work. The lifesaving motif still prevailed in the club's decorations: There was a liturgical lifeboat in the room where the club initiations were held.

About this time a large ship was wrecked off the coast, and the hired crews brought in boatloads of cold, wet and half-drowned people. They were dirty and sick, and some of them had black skin, and some of them had yellow skin. The beautiful new club was in chaos. So the property committee immediately had a shower built outside the club, where the victims of the shipwreck could be cleaned up before coming inside.

After the next meeting, there was a split in the club membership. Most of the members wanted to stop the club's lifesaving activities because they were unpleasant and a hindrance to the normal social life of the club. Some members insisted on lifesaving as their primary purpose and pointed out that they were still called a lifesaving station. But they were finally voted down and told that if they wanted to save lives of all various kinds of people who were shipwrecked in those waters, they could begin their own lifesaving station down the coast. They did.

As the years went by, the new station experienced the same changes that occurred in the old. It evolved into a club, and yet another lifesaving station was founded.

History continued to repeat itself, and if you visit that seacoast today, you will find a number of exclusive clubs along the shore. Shipwrecks are frequent in those waters, but most of the people drown.

Our purpose in life, according to the obvious moral of this parable, does not consist of hob-nobbing with our friends, going to school, graduating, finding a job, getting married, having children, sending them to school and so on. If we see only these parts of life, we will bog down continually. We need to see beyond all that.

When William Carey heard the strong call of the Lord to go to India in the late eighteenth century, his wife, Dorothy, resisted his decision and refused to go with him. He knew he could not disobey God, so he chose to go on even if she would not. The ship pulled away from the dock and sailed away, leaving her behind.

Then something on board broke down and the ship had to return to port for repairs. During the delay Dorothy reconsidered and chose to go to India with her husband. Later, however, she lost all ability to cope in India and suffered a mental breakdown. Carey was left to care for the children alone.

William Carey spent many years in India serving his Lord, and they were not easy ones. He paid an extremely high price to follow Jesus. His list of personal problems went on and on—but he saw beyond the pain and remembered the purpose of his life. Carey, whose challenge to the Church helped to found "the Baptist Society for Propagating the Gospel Among the Heathen" in 1792 (later the Baptist Missionary Society), and with his extensive contributions in linguistics and Bible translation, is known today as the father of modern missions.

Just a Bunch of Sheep

Throughout the Bible human beings are compared to sheep. Do you remember what one of the predominant characteristics of sheep is? They stray quite a bit. If left to our own devices and if we do not watch our hearts diligently, we, too, will always head the wrong way. It may take months or even years, but eventually our actions will follow the direction of our hearts. We will find every reason under the sun to justify our actions and choices until finally we are out of the battle, no longer serving or even following the Lord.

They say cars are designed with a built-in obsolescence factor—to run well for a few years, then begin to break down and become obsolete. Manufacturers hope the consumer will return to the dealership after a few years and begin the process all over again. In the human heart there is a built-in obsolescence factor, too. It does not matter how powerful and influential you are, how much education you have, how self-controlled or holy you consider yourself—your heart, if you do not guard it, will break down.

I have seen this principle played out too often in individuals' lives and in the Church at large. Many churches have drifted from the heart of the One they call Lord and Master. Now, instead of making it a priority to rescue the lost millions of the world from a Christless eternity, their programs revolve around themselves. They put their own agenda—whether buildings or staff or special programs—as first priority in their budgets. Missions falls somewhere down the list.

I met with a couple recently who talked with me about their calling as missionaries to France. After sharing in churches for two years, they were still unable to raise even seventy percent of the support they needed to enable them to get to France.

Proverbs 24:11–12 warns us:

> Rescue those being led away to death; hold back those staggering toward slaughter. If you say, "But we knew nothing about this," does not he who weighs the heart perceive it? Does not he who guards your life know it? Will he not repay each person according to what he has done?

Not long ago I spoke in a church that was involved to a limited extent in missions. After the meeting I had a bite to eat with the couple who had been our contact for this meeting. Our conversation lasted well into the night.

"You know, Brother K. P.," the husband told me, "I never really understood what's happening in the Church with regard to missions until I read your books. Our church offers solid, Bible-based teaching. In fact, it's one of the best Bible-teaching churches in the region. But with all this knowledge, I am sad to tell you we are spending more money on our own social programs than on missions!"

I do not want to make a big case out of this or pass judgment on anyone, much less the Church at large. But I do want to ask one question: Have the hearts of the members of the Body of Christ wandered so far from the reality of what is happening that they are impossible to bring back?

Our tendency as horizontally oriented humans is to forget the war going on behind the scenes and interpret everything in our lives through the filter of our five senses—what we see, hear, smell, touch and taste. Anything that has to do with these senses is our first approach to solving problems. Circumstances dictate how we feel and what we do. And we think in terms of ourselves rather than in terms of the purpose God has given us as believers. We have strayed from the focus of our hearts.

But we are not created for time. We are created for eternity. Our lives right now are little classrooms in which we are learning to be conformed to the image of the Lord Jesus Christ (Romans 8:29). And why did Jesus come into this world? What did He live for? "To seek and to save what was lost" (Luke 19:10).

Everything else in life becomes incidental when we gain this focus. Clothes, food, hairstyle, makeup, bank account, education, degrees, plans, ambition, spouse, children— none of these can possibly be the most important thing in life. The more we become like Christ, the more we, like Him, will make world evangelism the top priority in our lives.

Shankar, a native missionary in North India, was born in a leper colony to parents who were themselves stricken with leprosy. In order to save Shankar from contracting the disease, Brother Thomas, one of the Gospel for Asia native missionary leaders, raised him in a home he had built for the children of lepers.

Shankar received a good education, and with it a chance to make a better life for himself. But during his time with Brother Thomas, Shankar gave his life to the Lord and received a call to full-time ministry.

Just before Shankar's graduation from Bible school, he told Brother Thomas, "I will work among my own people, the lepers, and tell them how the Lord has changed my life. I will tell them how He can save them."

Today Shankar has laid down everything he has gained—his education and chance for a better life—to live and work as a missionary in the leper colonies of India. He did not lose his focus but set his heart on being a follower of Jesus.

I urge you to examine your own heart. Look at the things you do and the activities you are involved in for the sake of the Lord. Ask yourself honestly, *Why am I doing this?* Search your heart. Be real with yourself.

Seeing the Big Picture

Apart from the things of the Lord, I believe there are two things we value most in our lives: 1) We want to feel important, and 2) We want to be part of something important. No one wants to waste his or her life. But when we are involved in any work for the Lord, it becomes difficult at times to keep sight of how our investment in His Kingdom is making a difference. Satan can use those busy times in our lives to breed discouragement and bitterness and render us ineffective in the work of the Lord.

We need to see the big picture of what the Lord is doing so that the enemy will not use our immediate struggles, frustrations, disappointments or the demands on our time to cause us to become discouraged. Let us not become sidetracked or myopic, our vision fogged. I plead with you to remember that life on earth, no matter where you are, has its struggles, conflicts and discouragements. Ask the Lord for the grace and maturity to look *beyond* the immediate (which tends to take precedence over everything else) to the lives of those people you are influencing through your obedience and service to Him.

Joseph had done nothing wrong and walked in purity and commitment. He was obedient to his parents and his brothers. What did he do wrong to be sold into slavery and thrown into prison for thirteen years? What did he do wrong to lose everything he called his own? The Bible gives no reason. Those thirteen years were crucial, though, for Joseph to be able to reign as governor over Egypt and save the Israelites—and his own family—from starvation.

The Body of Christ reminds me of an elephant. Did you know that the elephant is the only creature who does not know how big his body is? His eyes are too small and he has two huge ears sticking out right beside them! So he walks around like a little animal, led by a small boy with a stick.

We are not able to see all that results from our efforts for the Lord, but let me encourage you to pursue what He has given you to do. What you are doing is more than just "work." We can be encouraged, knowing by faith that God in His mercy is able to use His Body to make an incredible impact on the world.

Restored to Tenderheartedness

During the heat of the Gulf War, I was as glued to the news as anyone. I kept my radio on as much as possible, straining for any new piece of information. Usually I spend my early morning hours preparing for my daily radio broadcast, but during the Gulf War I had a hard time concentrating.

As believers committed to reaching the lost, you and I are given more information about what is going on in the world today than ever before. We know more about Muslims, Hindus, Buddhists and other religious groups than the generations of believers who went before us. But let me ask you a question: How seriously do you take this information? The war we deal with on a daily basis—the battle that rages for the souls of men and women like you and me—is infinitely more serious than any war on earth.

When a Scud missile hit a military barracks during the war, killing 28 soldiers and wounding hundreds, America was shaken by the news. It shocked and moved the White House. The media could talk of nothing else. But does it move us to think that *more than one billion Muslims living in the world today do not know the love of Christ? That eighty thousand people are slipping into hell every 24 hours?*

I remember a particular victory won by the anti-Iraq forces. After hearing the details I walked calmly back to my desk to resume my studies. Then the conviction of the Lord came on me so strongly that I had to sit down. The reality of what I had heard hit me with full force. It was more than jet fighters and a few missiles. It was the fate of thousands of Muslims, whom I saw suddenly as the Lord did—desperately lost.

Is it nothing to you that these people are dying and going to hell? the Lord asked me.

Then I realized that I had not thought about the eternal implications of the news I had heard or spent even one minute to stop and pray that these people would have a chance to come to the Lord. Although I had heard news of the deaths of some of them, still I had gone about my business.

The Lord spoke strongly to my heart that day. I could only repent of my attitude.

Somewhere along the way many of us have become so familiar with certain kinds of information that our hearts have become hardened and cold. Here are the questions we should ask ourselves: Does my heart still beat with the same tenderness and passion for the dying world? Are there tears in my eyes for the lost and dying millions? When I hear news of the world around me, does my heart break for those who are going to hell? Do I get up in the morning to spend time with the Lord and pray for the lost?

I have to come continually before the Lord and ask, "Lord, am I getting too used to it all? Do I simply get up before congregations and say the same things over and over? Or are the burden and vision still fresh in my heart?"

No Price Is Too High

In the normal course of human nature, things never improve. We begin to take the things of the Lord casually. We find all sorts of reasons why our thinking is correct and why we should justify ourselves and our behavior. And unless we allow the Holy Spirit to renew our hearts and minds continually, deterioration will set in. It is like putting sand into the gears of a machine. They still crank, but the grinding noise is constant and the machine must work harder for anything to happen.

With the many needs and opportunities on the mission field, please do not let your involvement stop with "I'm doing the best I can." As followers of Jesus, the things we do—whether praying, giving, sending or going—determine to a great extent what happens on the other side of the world. So I encourage you to search your heart. Is the passion still there? Is your heart broken?

No one can restore that freshness or passion for you. You must come before the Lord and allow Him to renew the focus of your heart.

Amy Carmichael was one who never lost her focus. One of the great pioneer missionaries to India, she wrote a book called *Things as They Are*. This is what she saw one night as she lay in bed:

> . . . I stood on a grassy sward, and at my feet a precipice broke sheer down into infinite space. I looked, but saw no bottom; only cloud shapes, black and furiously coiled, and great shadow-shrouded hollows, and unfathomable depths. Back I drew, dizzy at the depth.
>
> Then I saw forms of people moving single file along the grass. They were making for the edge. There was a woman with a baby in her arms and another little child holding onto her dress. She was on the very verge. Then I saw that she was blind. She lifted her foot for the next step . . . it trod air. She was over, and the children over with her. Oh, the cry as they went over!
>
> Then I saw more streams of people flowing from all quarters. All were blind, stone blind; all made straight for the precipice edge. There were shrieks as they suddenly knew themselves falling, and a tossing up of helpless arms, catching, clutching at empty air. But some went over quietly, and fell without a sound.

Sentries were set at intervals, but the gaps were too great. Why, Carmichael agonized, was no one stopping them at the edge?

Then I saw, like a little picture of peace, a group of people under some trees with their backs turned towards the gulf. They were making daisy chains. Sometimes when a piercing shriek cut the quiet air and reached them, it disturbed them and they thought it a rather vulgar noise. And if one of their number started up and wanted to go and do something to help, then all the others would pull that one down. "Why should you get so excited about it? You must wait for a definite call to go! You haven't finished your daisy chain yet. It would be really selfish," they said, "to leave us to finish the work alone."

Another group wanted to send out more sentries but could find few candidates. One sentry, a girl, was compelled to take her furlough though there was no one to take her place.

Once a child caught at a tuft of grass that grew at the very brink of the gulf; it clung convulsively, and it called—but nobody seemed to hear. Then the roots of the grass gave way, and with a cry the child went over, its two little hands still holding tight to the torn-off bunch of grass. And the girl who longed to be back in her gap thought she heard the little one cry, and she sprang up and wanted to go; at which they reproved her, reminding her that no one is necessary anywhere; the gap would be well taken care of, they knew. And then they sang a hymn.

Then through the hymn came another sound like the pain of a million broken hearts wrung out in one full drop, one sob. And a horror of great darkness was upon me, for I knew what it was—the Cry of the Blood.

Then thundered a voice, the voice of the Lord. "And He said, 'What hast thou done? The voice of thy brother's blood crieth unto me from the ground.'"

The . . . darkness still shuddered and shivered about me. . . .

What does it matter, after all? It has gone on for years; it will go on for years. Why make such a fuss about it?

God forgive us! God arouse us! Shame us out of our callousness! Shame us out of our sin!

Many in the Church in the West criticized Amy Carmichael for writing like this, telling her she was condemning them as though they were the worst of heathens.

But unless we think carefully, make deliberate decisions and allow the Lord to break our hearts continually, we will walk in the way of all flesh.

When was the last time you wept because your heart was burdened for those dying who have never heard the name of Jesus? When was the last time you spent an evening praying over a world map? Let us not lose the focus of our heart and leave the battle because we are unwilling to live with the reality that half the world is still waiting to hear the Gospel.

The cry of the lost world comes loud and desperate to our ears. Let us be willing to hear and respond to it. He is waiting to do major things through us, but we must bring our hearts back into focus. When they are, we can no longer live for ourselves—our own needs and desires, struggles and disappointments. Instead we will be ready to make sacrifices, laying down our very lives so that others will know Jesus.

In the next chapter we will be looking at four attacks Satan uses against believers whose hearts are set on winning the lost world for Jesus.

Knowing the Enemy

Imagine that you and I are allowed to observe a meeting held for all the powers of darkness. The setting is a huge conference hall, and in the audience are millions of demons gathered from the corners of the earth by Satan himself. As they enter the hall, they whisper to one another: "What's going on? What is this meeting about? What is our Master's agenda?"

They look around, and there on the wall in huge letters are written these words: *"And this gospel of the kingdom will be preached in the whole world as a testimony to all nations, and then the end will come"* (Matthew 24:14).

The prince of darkness approaches the podium to address his army.

"Do you understand," he thunders, indicating the words of Jesus Christ written on the wall, "that when this Gospel of our enemy is preached to the whole world, it means *our* end as well?"

94

Satan is keenly aware of what will happen to him and his legions of demons when the end comes. He already knows what is written in the final chapter: He will be forever tormented in the lake of fire. It is only a matter of time before the appointed moment when his doom is sealed by God.

The appointed moment is also mentioned when Jesus was about to cast the demons out of the men in the country of the Gadarenes. The demons cried out, "What do you want with us, Son of God? Have you come here to torture us *before the appointed time?*" (Matthew 8:29, italics added).

A short time is all the enemy has, which will be cut even shorter by the preaching of the Gospel to all nations. As we reach our generation for the Lord, we hasten His coming as well as the demise of the devil. If we are able to mobilize the entire Body of Christ all over the world to move out and witness, it will be only a few years before Jesus returns.

Do you think the devil is happy over this? We are told that "he is filled with fury, because he knows that his time is short" (Revelation 12:12). I can assure you that he does his utmost to extend that time in any way possible. In fact, those of us who have heard the call of eternity and committed ourselves to pray, give and go to reach the lost world have set ourselves up (whether we realize it or not) for direct, face-to-face confrontation with the powers of darkness.

For years now at Gospel for Asia, we have seen how those preparing to join our home team staff face serious attack once they make their decision to come. Some experience health problems. Others deal with emotional turbulence. And most face opposition, sometimes severe, from relatives and friends.

We routinely tell anyone who has been called to join our staff, "Now that you've made a decision to join this ministry, we want to put you on the alert that there will be many battles to face. You will experience attacks and opposition to your decision. You need to be prepared and pray, along with us, for the Lord's protection."

The battle we face with the powers of darkness is an ongoing one. If there is anything good to be said about the devil, it is that he is a hard worker. He never rests, never sleeps, never goes on vacation. He works all the time.

So as long as our hearts are committed to serving the Lord and helping advance His Kingdom on earth, we will always face opposition from the enemy. Whenever we are serving the Lord, especially when it comes to reaching people who live in lands ruled for centuries by demonic powers and principalities, you can be sure we will find ourselves in the very heat of the battle.

Supernatural Networking

Recently I heard about five hundred Hindus in North India who gave their lives to Christ and were baptized after watching a film on the life of Jesus. Imagine what a stir this caused among the ranks of demons who suddenly lost their power over these people! Here is a possible scenario:

"What's wrong with you?" a demon leader demands of his gang. "Why did you let this happen?"

"What can we do?" they whine. "We were doing our best to keep them in darkness, but these missionaries brought in that projector and film, and they keep going from village to village with it. And they do so much praying! They don't give us any rest."

The head demon checks out this Gospel for Asia outfit and finds out that somewhere in America—in Carrollton, Texas—funds are being raised to support these missionaries.

So the commander of the Carrollton region is alerted: "A group of people in your territory is causing us big trouble in India. Do what you can to stop them!"

Soon the Carrollton commander has a file on each staff member of Gospel for Asia. He knows every name, every address, every car that is driven, every book that is read, every weakness, every fear, every struggle and how each staff member can be attacked most effectively.

Does this sound outlandish? It shouldn't. Even human beings have the capability of comprehensive communication. I discovered recently that everyone in India, even in the most remote village, can get CNN. All they have to do is pay to get it hooked up. The Internet computer network has made the information revolution accessible to most of the globe. And a recent cover story of *Newsweek* showed a photograph of a Samburu warrior in a desolate region of northern Kenya with a spear in one hand and a cellular telephone in the other.

Believe me, if human beings with our finite, low-level minds have the genius for this kind of communication, there is no doubt Satan can make a connection between what happens on the mission field and your personal commitment to give and pray for missions. His ultimate goal is to do everything in his power to lead men and women away from Christ and take them to hell.

Jesus calls Satan "the prince of this world" (John 12:31). The apostle John tells us that the whole world is lying in the lap of the wicked one (see 1 John 5:19). Political systems, religious hierarchies, financial institutions, educational and banking systems—everything on earth can be manipulated by the enemy to lead men and women away from the living God and keep them in bondage.

He is working on believers, too, particularly in our areas of vulnerability. You sometimes experience tensions and conflicts with those who are closest to you—your children, your spouse, your close relatives. You find a tendency toward friction in your church, in the Christian organization you work with, in your prayer group or home fellowship. Because we live and work together as human beings, these things occur naturally. They also represent areas of vulnerability to demonic attack.

The soldiers who go to war are the ones who get wounded. People who drive cars are the ones who have accidents. The families who have children are the ones who have struggles in raising them. Those who are alive are the ones who get headaches and illnesses. Only when you are dead, lying in your coffin under the earth, will you face no problems!

Jesus had plenty of problems with His disciples. They squabbled among themselves as to who was the greatest, and fought for their future positions around His throne. Peter ran off at the mouth without thinking. Judas was ready to do anything for money—even betray his Master.

Particularly in the process of doing our very best to build the Lord's Kingdom, we face problems. We can expect it.

I want to point out four areas where the enemy can easily attack those whose hearts are committed to reaching the lost world. I want to share these because I believe that as you are forewarned and take these to heart, you will be strengthened and encouraged to stand firm in the days to come.

Burning the Barn Down

One attack of the enemy is *tempting us to major on minor issues*. And for those who are involved in any way in winning the lost world, the attack of the enemy is more severe and direct. He takes advantage of the problems we face and, like a balloon, blows them up bigger and bigger so that our vision of everything else is blocked. Suddenly all we see are the problems.

A Christian organization I heard about was attacked in the press. The problem stemmed from a disagreement between two board members and the leader of this organization. The people fueling the fire were so-called Christian brothers who went to the media with their complaints and in so doing undermined the work of God. The problem was publicized; no mention was made of the 99 good things this organization does.

The enemy used these men to blow the problem out of proportion. Not only did the annual income of this organization drop nearly a million dollars, but great damage was done to millions of suffering people around the world as a result.

This is what Satan does: He takes small things and makes them big. The pastor of a church may have said or done something that caused a misunderstanding. A clique is formed, people blow the problem out of proportion and the church, instead of dealing with it, divides.

Some time ago a woman called Gospel for Asia and told me that she and her husband could no longer support our organization. When I asked why, she said it was because someone had told her GFA had become liberal. I asked how she had come to such a conclusion.

"Well," she responded, "I found out that GFA workers do not use the King James Version of the Bible."

"I'm sorry, they don't," I replied.

"You've deceived me!" she exclaimed. "I can't support your work any longer."

Then I asked her, "Are you aware that your missionary in Thailand doesn't speak English? You realize, of course, that the King James Bible is in English?"

My point here is not to argue about the King James Version, which I love. But this woman allowed Satan to take a small problem and blow it out of proportion; and as a result she decided to give up her commitment to support a native missionary. (Later she changed her mind.)

The enemy will highlight specific failures, even the smallest shortcomings, of leaders of Christian organizations, pastors, church elders and those with whom you work and fellowship. Be on your guard against focusing on just that problem alone. If you do, you will be blinded to the total picture, and this can be very dangerous.

Jesus encountered such blindness. The Pharisees, who caught Jesus' disciples eating their food without washing their hands according to the Jewish law, blocked out everything else Jesus taught and focused on this one apparent failure. Or when Jesus healed the sick on the Sabbath, the Pharisees jumped on Him and said He could not be from God since He worked on the Sabbath. These Pharisees were extremely conscientious when it came to religion. They gave tithes, prayed and fasted. But they left out mercy, kindness and love. Jesus told them, "Go and learn what this means: 'I desire mercy, not sacrifice'" (Matthew 9:13).

There seems to be an increasing tendency today for believers to search out the smallest hint of anything negative in Christian organizations, ministries and local churches. Church-hoppers and self-proclaimed spiritual vigilantes are on the increase.

I heard recently about a church that experienced tremendous growth. A seven-thousand-seat auditorium was built to handle the continuous influx of new members. But now that building sits with many empty pews. Why? Because the leadership of the church was accused of several mistakes. No one could corroborate these mistakes, but most of the members left overnight.

When you are active in a local body of believers, when you support your local church and pastor, and when you pray for Christian ministries, you will soon find problems. But do not forsake your friendships, pack your bags and walk off. You do not abandon a true friend when he has problems; you stay and pray with him. We need to develop this character in our churches, prayer fellowships and ministries so that our brothers and sisters do not suffer needlessly.

I have heard a saying: *You don't burn the barn down just to kill a rat.* If you have a barn, you expect to find a few rats. But you do not demolish the place just to kill them; you target the rats.

When you face a problem that looms large in your vision, keep two things in mind: First, pray about it. Commit yourself to pray for your leaders, for the ministries you know, for the church, for the pastor and for those people who are stirring up the problem. Then focus your heart on the 99 percent of good that is happening. Determine to see the problem for what it really is—in light of everything else and not standing by itself.

Let us purpose to see the problems we deal with in the total picture of what God is doing. And even when we are faced with injustices, even when our rights are violated, let us say with Paul, "What does it matter? The important thing is that in every way, whether from false motives or true, Christ is preached. And because of this I rejoice" (Philippians 1:18).

Rationalizing Our Desire to Follow the Crowd

The second attack Satan wages against followers of Jesus is *tempting us to become self-centered by rationalization.* Everybody is doing it, we reason, so it must be O.K. We adopt a herd mentality.

I heard a story on the radio recently. A man approaching a big bridge in his car saw another man standing close to the edge, looking down into the river. He stopped his car and went over to the man, apparently hoping to counsel him to save his life. In the end, though, both men jumped off the bridge to their deaths.

This is a perfect illustration of human nature. Our flesh never looks for what it can do for God's Kingdom, but for what it can get for itself. As a result we are easily swayed to become self-centered. All we have to do is rationalize a bit.

An interesting event is recorded in John 21 that took place after Jesus was resurrected, when Peter decided to go back to fishing. "[The disciples] said, 'We'll go with you'" (John 21:3). How easily influenced these disciples were by Peter's decision!

We are not much different. It is easy to rationalize our actions, our decisions, even our thoughts. But when your heart becomes discouraged, when doubts rise in your mind, when you are tired and want out of the battle, remember that it does not matter what happens to anyone else. Your only concern is to follow the Lord.

Peter was used by Satan to pull the disciples away from their commitment to Jesus and run after the fishing nets and boats again. I pray that none of us will become an instrument in the hand of the enemy to cause a brother or sister to stumble.

We talked in the last chapter about William Carey, who answered the call of the Lord in the late eighteenth century to go to India. But when he shared the burden on his heart with the elders in his congregation, their response was, "Sit down, young man. If God wants to save those heathens, He'll find someone else." Carey could easily have rationalized that he should listen to the elders. Instead he decided to obey the Lord's calling alone.

What about Daniel and his friends? They stood alone, captives in a foreign land. They chose to follow God's law and faced isolation, persecution, even the loss of their lives.

What about Enoch? Genesis 5 records a long list of names, and in the middle of the list we read, "Enoch walked with God" (verse 22). All alone, it seems.

Jeremiah faced four decades of prophecy, laments, rejection, misunderstandings and persecution, and had to stand all alone.

Jesus also stood alone. And to His disciples He said, "I am sending you out like lambs among wolves" (Luke 10:3).

You must not look for approval from anybody as you seek to build the Lord's Kingdom. Sometimes you must set your face against the cold wind and walk all alone.

The enemy will use many voices around you to attack you so that you begin to question your calling. You will be tempted to rationalize what you hear. What are you to do, after all? Your father is against you, your mother, your brothers and sisters, the whole congregation, everyone. The Lord must not be calling you after all.

But take a lesson from Joshua and Caleb. When Moses sent the twelve spies into Canaan, the majority of the group concluded that the children of Israel should not go into the land. Only Joshua and Caleb said, "We can go in and take it," even though they were the minority and no one would listen. People even picked up stones to stone them. Jesus told us our lives with Him would lead down a narrow road. Be watchful and alert so that you are not deceived by the majority.

Do not forget that Jesus' own brothers came to snatch Him away, saying He was "out of his mind" (Mark 3:21; see John 7:5). Jesus said: "Anyone who loves his father or mother more than me is not worthy of me; anyone who loves his son or daughter more than me is not worthy of me" (Matthew 10:37).

As we follow Christ, our closest relatives—even our parents—might oppose our decision. Jesus said:

> "Do not suppose that I have come to bring peace to the earth. I did not come to bring peace, but a sword. For I have come to turn
>
> "'a man against his father,
>   a daughter against her mother,
> a daughter-in-law against her mother-in-law—
>   a man's enemies will be the members of his own household.'"
>
> Matthew 10:34–36

But we are called to keep our allegiance to God's revealed Word, to obey Him and follow Him.

This is true especially in the Muslim and Hindu communities. Many young people who come to the Lord refuse to worship in the mosque or bow down before idols in the temples, and for this they are killed. They are willing to take a stand against the deeply entrenched family system.

You must also know the call of Christ beyond the shadow of a doubt if you are to hear the call and abandon your life to Him. Do not let the majority become the tool of the enemy to deceive you. That does not mean we should not listen to the wisdom of those in our prayer fellowship or congregation. The Bible tells us that "for lack of guidance a nation falls, but many advisers make victory sure" (Proverbs 11:14). But this is one of the areas where we need to be extremely watchful of the enemy's tactics.

Not Recognizing the Fiery Darts

The third way the enemy attacks us is by *tempting us to forget we have an enemy*. Satan's ultimate desire is not to withhold funds or stop programs from being carried out. His plan is to make believers ineffective in the work of the Kingdom.

As followers of Jesus in a fallen world, we are not immune to the devil's attacks. No one is exempt from these struggles, especially those serving the Lord on the front lines. Satan hurls his fiery darts at us constantly, using the tiniest problem to waste our precious time. We face discouragement, sorrow, misunderstanding and disappointment, and may not even recognize these as the fiery darts of the enemy.

But Paul tells us we are in a spiritual war, and to stand firm and pray always (Ephesians 6:12–13, 18). Unless we stay in the battle, we can easily get crushed by the enemy.

And we need to realize how important it is to pray for God's protection over one another.

We have no need to be afraid of the enemy's schemes. We are told to "resist the devil, and he will flee from you" (James 4:7). John encourages us, "You, dear children, are from God and have overcome [evil spirits], because the one who is in you is greater than the one who is in the world" (1 John 4:4).

God is never troubled by the lack of money or ideas. His greatest purpose is to find people. "The eyes of the LORD range throughout the earth to strengthen those whose hearts are fully committed to him" (2 Chronicles 16:9). It is individuals—you and I—whom God has chosen to change the course of this generation. Sometimes we forget this, but Satan has never forgotten it. He sees the servants of the Lord as an awesome threat and does his best to make us as ineffective as possible.

Let me share some encouraging words by an unknown author that came across my desk recently:

> The Lord has given every man his work. It is his business to do it, and the devil's business to hinder him if he can. And as sure as God has given you a work to do, Satan will try to hinder you.
>
> My dear Christian friend, *keep at your work*. Do not flinch because the lion roars; do not stop to stone the devil's dogs; do not fool away your time chasing the devil's rabbits. Do your work. Let liars lie, let religious sectarians quarrel, let corporations resolve, let editors publish, and come what may, let the devil do his worst; but see to it that *nothing* hinders you from fulfilling the work God has given you.
>
> Keep at your work. Let your aim be as steady as a star. Let the world brawl and babble and bubble. Keep at your work. You may be assaulted, wronged, insulted, slandered, wounded and rejected; you may be abused by foes, forsaken by friends and despised and rejected of men, but see to it with steadfast determination, with unfaltering zeal, that

you pursue the great purpose of your life and the object of
your being, until at last you can say, "I have run the race
. . . I have finished the work which thou gavest me to do."

Succumbing to Our Natural Thoughts

Finally, one of the strongest attacks of the enemy against
believers is *tempting us to forget our need to exercise faith in
God*. Hebrews 11:6 says, "Without faith it is impossible to
please God."

There are times in our lives when we have more questions than answers. Our emotions are dry and cold. Nothing gives us reason to get excited or happy about serving
God. What do we do?

Times like these are part of the battle. They are when
"the righteous will live by his faith" (Habakkuk 2:4). In
every battle we face, we need to keep in mind that faith is
the key that helps us overcome the world and the enemy.
"This is the victory that has overcome the world, even our
faith" (1 John 5:4).

After spying out the land of Canaan, Joshua and Caleb
said, "Let's go!" Caleb in particular was a radical revolutionary who told Moses and the people of Israel, "We
should go up and take possession of the land, for we can
certainly do it" (Numbers 13:30).

What did the other ten spies say? "This is impossible!
We can't do it. We saw giants in the land, and we ourselves
are grasshoppers in comparison" (see Numbers 13:33).

Forty-five years later, when it was finally time for Israel
to enter the land of Canaan, Caleb at age 85 was still ready
to go and possess his inheritance:

> "I am still as strong today as the day Moses sent me out;
> I'm just as vigorous to go out to battle now as I was then.
> Now give me this hill country that the LORD promised me

that day. . . . The LORD helping me, I will drive [the Anakites] out just as he said."

Joshua 14:11–12

Caleb lived his whole life following the Lord. When he saw the land of Canaan, he had no doubt that the children of Israel could possess it—not because he was confident in their might, but because he was confident in God's ability to go beyond any weakness or frailty. God honored Caleb's faith and gave him a special inheritance in the Promised Land because, as Moses told him, "You have followed the LORD my God wholeheartedly" (Joshua 14:9).

If you know anything about faith, you know there is something innate in us that works *against* faith, even in the most knowledgeable theologian or the most powerful preacher. "The man without the Spirit does not accept the things that come from the Spirit of God, for they are foolishness to him" (1 Corinthians 2:14). No matter how much we read and memorize the Bible, our natural mind always comes up with some argument against God's way of doing things. This is why exercising faith is so important.

The Lord makes a clear distinction between His thoughts and ours:

> Let the wicked forsake his way and the evil man his thoughts. Let him turn to the LORD, and he will have mercy on him, and to our God, for he will freely pardon. "For my thoughts are not your thoughts, neither are your ways my ways," declares the LORD. "As the heavens are higher than the earth, so are my ways higher than your ways and my thoughts than your thoughts."
>
> Isaiah 55:7–9

An important part of spiritual warfare involves dealing with our natural thoughts, those that work against faith.

Paul exhorted the believers in Corinth—and us today as well:

> For though we live in the world, we do not wage war as the world does. The weapons we fight with are not the weapons of the world. On the contrary, they have divine power to demolish strongholds. We demolish arguments and every pretension that sets itself up against the knowledge of God, and we take captive every thought to make it obedient to Christ.
>
> 2 Corinthians 10:3–5

When Elisha the prophet was serving the Lord in Israel, a powerful Syrian captain named Naaman came to him. He had heard that Elisha could heal him of his leprosy. But Elisha made a strange requirement: "Go, wash yourself seven times in the Jordan, and your flesh will be restored and you will be cleansed" (2 Kings 5:10).

Naaman became angry when he heard this. The word in the King James is *wroth*, and it translates to mean that he burst out in anger. Naaman probably spewed out a stream of vulgarities.

Why was he so angry? Verse 11 records Naaman's explanation: "I thought that he would surely come out to me and stand and call on the name of the LORD his God, wave his hand over the spot and cure me of my leprosy." Naaman was not a small man in the kingdom of Syria, and what the prophet had asked him to do was insulting.

No matter what God says, our own thoughts will either try to get the job done, or say it cannot be done, or say it is not God's will for it to be done, or say that is not the way He works. Our thoughts will always come up with something to counteract what God asks us to do.

What can we do about our wayward minds? First we must search our hearts and make sure nothing is keeping us from uniting our hearts with one another. The Bible tells us that "if two of you on earth agree about anything you ask for, it will be done for you by my Father in heaven" (Matthew 18:19). The other important thing to keep in mind is what Jesus told us in Mark 11:24: "Therefore I tell you, whatever you ask for in prayer, believe that you have received it, and it will be yours." So many have used this verse out of context over the years that we have a tendency to write it off. But that verse is in your Bible and mine as well!

It sounds simplistic, doesn't it, just to *believe!* As a matter of fact, it sounds more like something an ignorant child would do rather than an educated adult.

When my daughter, Sarah, was very small, her older cousins had great fun with her during our regular visits to my home village in India. They discovered that she believed anything they told her! Soon it happened regularly that Sarah would come running home with some wild story she had heard from a cousin, which she believed with all her heart. She did not know *not* to believe it.

And in terms of the Kingdom of God, this is exactly what Jesus is telling us to do—to believe as a child believes: "I tell you the truth, unless you change and become like little children, you will never enter the kingdom of heaven" (Matthew 18:3).

When you pray for an unsaved loved one, for revival in your church, for a spiritual breakthrough in Islamic countries, for the unsaved to be reached with the Gospel, remember what Jesus said: "Believe that you have received it." When God told Abraham he would have a son, Abraham not only believed it but began to thank God. Later on he received his son.

I encourage you to exercise your faith actively in what God is able to do. Go beyond your natural thoughts and reactions. Trust Him, in obedience to what His Word says, for miracles far greater than what your mind could ever imagine.

The Victory That Overcomes the World

I agree there is no point in investing our time and energy to study the intricate strategies of the devil. Yet for those of us who serve the Lord and are committed to His purposes, I want to stress how important it is to be aware that our lives make a powerful impact on the spiritual world.

It is vitally important for us to remember that our walk and service to the Lord are not a normal, nine-to-five, five-day-a-week job for which we clock in and clock out. We must realize, by the very nature of our commitment to the Lord, that we may face attacks and problems anytime. Our safeguard is to be aware daily of these attacks. And as we take up the weapons of our warfare as described in Ephesians 6, we will be overcomers in this battle: "Put on the full armor of God, so that when the day of evil comes, you may be able to stand your ground, and after you have done everything, to stand" (Ephesians 6:13).

In the next chapter, the final chapter of this section, we will look at the greatest weapon in our arsenal.

The Weapon That Guarantees Victory

I remember a point in my life when I realized I needed to pray more. An hour seemed like a good place to start.

Early the next morning I woke up and, after making sure I was awake, knelt by the side of the bed and started to pray. I poured out my heart to the Lord, praying about everything I could think of. When I had finished, I figured at least 45 minutes had gone by, if not the whole hour.

I looked at my clock. I had prayed for only four minutes! But I had prayed about everything I knew. What would I do for the next 56 minutes?

Suddenly prayer was not as simple as it seemed. Have you ever felt that way?

Yet I cannot stress enough how vital it is to develop a consistent prayer life. Without prayer your walk with the Lord will lack substance and credibility. With prayer your walk with the Lord will be victorious, since prayer is the weapon of warfare that guarantees victory.

And in prayer you will find God's heart for the more than two billion lives who are still unreached with the Gospel. God created every person in His image with an eternal soul, yet everyone who does not know Jesus is bound in chains of sin heading toward hell, many not even knowing there is a name to call upon for salvation. God is searching for those who will stand in the gap on their behalf and intercede for their souls.

What Does Prayer Do?

When was the last time you considered the implications of what serious prayer will accomplish in your life?

Prayer Gets You Alone with God

Unless we are spending time with the Lord, we cannot understand what it means to follow Christ. We are easily deceived into thinking that a few good choruses and hymns, a dynamic sermon and an outstanding church program are where it is at.

We are wrong. One of the highest items on God's agenda throughout the Bible is to get His people alone with Him. Jacob ran from God for twenty years or more before God met him alone. Only then could He make him Israel.

When you spend time alone with the Lord, you cannot be a phony. When it is just God and you, you come face-to-face with yourself and your sins. With everyone else you can argue sin away, or smile and cover it up. Only when you are alone with God can cleansing and purification take place.

You may say, "Me—pray for a few weeks or days, or even for an hour? You're joking, right?"

But God is in the business of making His children into the likeness of His Son. Romans 8:29 says, "Those God foreknew he also predestined to be conformed to the likeness of his Son." But He cannot do this until He has some time with us.

When you have truly given your life to the Lord, it no longer belongs to you. You have died to yourself. Now Jesus can live His life through you and you can take every concern straight to Him: "Jesus, I need to talk to this person about You, but I don't know what to say. Could You please help me?"

It is simple when you are in tune with God. You will find yourself like the man who dug deep and anchored the foundation for his house on bedrock. No matter what circumstances may bluster your way, you are solid because you are anchored to the Rock.

And if you fail to lay that foundation? You may have the most attractive house in the neighborhood, but if serious winds and rains come, it will be gone in a moment. "That idiot!" the neighbors will say. "He built his house with no foundation."

Please do not misunderstand me. Even if your prayer life is inconsistent and you cry out to the Lord, He is merciful and will hear you. But if you develop a habit of praying and spending time with the Lord, you will realize how precious that cord of communication is. Getting to know Jesus and loving Him are not one-day things. The more you know Him, the more you will love Him. And the more you love Him, the more He will revolutionize your life, and the more you will live in the light of eternity.

Prayer Moves the Hand of God

Prayer is one of the most difficult jobs you will ever undertake—but it is the quickest way to get anything done. What would otherwise take fifty years of struggle can be accomplished in five, if the battles are first won in prayer. I have seen this happen over and over on the front lines of the mission field.

When you read about the lives of the New Testament Christians, you find that when they were threatened or harassed, when they faced struggles or problems, they met immediately for prayer. And the book of Acts records this about their prayer meeting: "After they prayed, the place where they were meeting was shaken. And they were all filled with the Holy Spirit and spoke the word of God boldly" (Acts 4:31).

These believers rooted their every action in prayer. They were filled with power to do the impossible and affected their community radically. Even though they were unlearned and uneducated with no special training, everyone knew they had spent time with Jesus (see Acts 4:13).

Do you ever say to yourself things like these:

"I'm so tired of the way my husband lives his life. I thought all these years that he was an honest man, but now I've found out his private life is not so wonderful."

"I'm frustrated with my wife's unwillingness to commit her life to the cause of God's Kingdom. I wish she wouldn't resist my efforts to pray and give to the Lord. I wish things would be different."

"I'm tired of trying to witness to my coworker. All he does is make fun of my faith and deliberately try to trap or test me. I wish he would change—or just leave."

What is your next step? Run out for the newest self-help book that will tell you how to make it work? Throughout the Bible one thing moved the hand of almighty God: prayer.

On many occasions Jesus spent an entire night in prayer, often after a day of hard work. The next day He would go out and minister to people in the strength of the Spirit.

The dynamite power that flowed through Him was a direct result of His contact with the Father.

Prayer Equips You for Battle

When I urge you to intercede for the lost, you know I am not talking about the phrase you may have added to your prayers at the dinner table as you were growing up: "Lord, please bless this food and bless our family—and save the heathens in Africa." No, I am talking about entering an incredible spiritual battle, making a deliberate choice to wage warfare against the powers of darkness for the release of souls who have no one else to fight for their deliverance.

Paul exhorts us in Ephesians 6 to use prayer as a weapon:

> Our struggle is not against flesh and blood, but against the rulers, against the authorities, against the powers of this dark world and against the spiritual forces of evil in the heavenly realms. Therefore put on the full armor of God. . . . And pray in the Spirit on all occasions with all kinds of prayers and requests. With this in mind, be alert and always keep on praying for all the saints.
>
> Ephesians 6:12–13, 18

We face tremendous opportunities today on the mission field. People's hearts are open to receive the Gospel and we are able to send workers into the most unreached areas. At the same time we face a great increase in opposition and persecution on the mission field. We also face self-centeredness and misunderstandings within the Body of Christ, which often hinder the willingness of the Church to give to missions.

We need to unite together to pray against the powers of darkness. They will not be defeated any other way. Spiritual breakthroughs will come not as we sit and wish for them to happen, but as we are on our knees.

Prayer Changes the Course of History

Do you realize that some of the history-changing revivals took place not through a massive effort of hundreds of people, but through a small handful who prayed and fasted? Whole nations have been changed because three, four or five people were willing to get on their knees before the living God.

I know of a community in India where more than sixty percent of the people came to Jesus Christ because a group of men prayed and fasted for two weeks before they opened their mouths to utter one word in the village. Prayer is what changes people, circumstances, nations and even history.

You may say, "I am not a mighty man or woman. I'm a weakling when it comes to prayer. What can I do?"

I will offer some suggestions in a moment, but first let me tell you this: When you are weak, when you stumble and fall, the cross of Christ becomes powerful! Jesus has told us, "My power is made perfect in weakness" (2 Corinthians 12:9). The men and women of God whose stories are recorded in the Bible are men and women who changed their circumstances. Realize that you are able, by God's grace, to change *your* circumstances.

Often we have a tendency to wait instead for our circumstances to change: "I'll be able to do something for God when my ship comes in." Did you send a ship out? You cannot guarantee that one will come in!

You may say, "I would fast and pray for Tibet if I had a little more physical strength." Or, "I'll think about ministry after I get married." Or, "I can focus on doing more when my problems at home are solved." Or, "I'll sell out everything to serve the Lord after my retirement."

You cannot live in the light of eternity with this attitude. But if you do not have a consistent prayer life, you cannot know the resources God has already given you. He has given you power, but the key to power is prayer "on all occasions" (Ephesians 6:18).

Cultivating a Richer Prayer Life

As a ministry Gospel for Asia is fairly young; at the time of this writing we are just past the fifteen-year mark. But wherever I go people ask me the secret to our growth. One organization even sent a delegate to our Dallas office to find out what was behind it. I walked with him through our office while we talked.

"Tell me, Brother K. P.," he said. "Which agency does your fundraising?"

"We have no agency," I replied, "although we're not against them. Some agencies are made up of godly people called by the Lord to help build His Kingdom."

He was a little confused. "Well, then, what do you have?"

"At the very beginning of our ministry, we started a Tuesday evening prayer meeting that has been going on ever since. We meet from seven until nine every Tuesday night. Also, our office staff arrives half an hour early three mornings a week to pray before the day begins. And on the first Friday of each month we meet for all-night prayer, which lasts until three or four in the morning. We spend more time praying than planning. We simply pray for everything that happens. If we have a need for something, we just pray."

We are not throwing out logical thought, of course. We need planning and budgeting. We need the best brainstorming sessions to learn how to share the message more effectively. But neglecting to bathe the ministry in prayer leaves us just workers, not worshipers. When we unite in prayer, there is incredible power.

It is not my intention to intimidate you into a prayer life or put you on some guilt trip. Prayer is not something we can legislate. It has to flow from each believer's heart to the Lord. At the same time, I cannot overemphasize how important prayer is. It is such a vital part of our lives as followers of Jesus that *no* excuse is good enough to keep us away from it!

Is prayer mandatory? *It is not.* We cannot create spirituality or put our brothers and sisters under bondage of guilt and legalism.

Is prayer mandatory? *It is!* How can we stay away from it if we are to follow Jesus seriously?

If you desire a fresh prayer life and are wondering how and where to start, let me offer a few suggestions that might help you find your way:

1. *Take some time to pray right now.* Humble yourself before the Lord Jesus. Tell Him of your desire to spend more time in His presence. Ask Him to help you know how to pray and what to pray about. This is the first major step you must take before anything else can happen.

2. As you begin to spend more time in prayer, *allow your heart to open up in worship to the Lord.* You need an individual life of worship, not just during the corporate worship time of your church.

What is worship? Literally it means to fall down prostrate before the Lord. When you begin to understand who God really is, you will worship Him. Find Bible verses that mention His names and what they mean. Use Scripture to pray, including many of the beautiful expressions in the Psalms. Sing songs to the Lord. If you do not know any songs or the ones you know do not seem to fit, make some up.

3. *Use some common resources to give you items for prayer.* Watch the news on TV if you do not know what is going on in the world. Get hold of a major newspaper and read the international section. Scribble down some notes about what is happening in Myanmar, Afghanistan or China.

Begin to pray for the needs of these nations. Put up a world map in your house. Get a copy of *Operation World* by Patrick Johnstone, which gives a tremendous amount of information on the spiritual condition of every country in the world. Subscribe to the newspaper published by Gospel for Asia, SEND!, and other missions publications. Make every report a matter of intercession.

Soon you will discover that thirty minutes, an hour or even two hours will not be enough to scratch the surface.

God in His incredible wisdom has ordained prayer to be the most powerful weapon of the Church. If He had chosen anything else, like preaching, singing, money or education, many of us could not participate in waging warfare. But prayer requires none of these things. It can take place anywhere, anytime and can be done by anyone. A housewife, a child, a grandfather, a corporate executive—all are able to impact the world and help change the destiny of millions.

It is to the personal price of reaching those millions that we now turn.

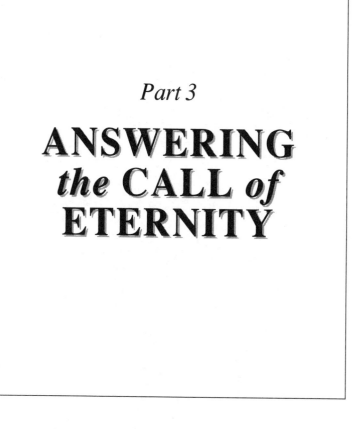

Part 3

ANSWERING *the* CALL *of* ETERNITY

Selling All for the Pearl

On August 27, 1990, at 6:10 A.M. my mother died. She was 84. Her last words were, "I am going to my Father's house." She loved the Lord deeply and walked closely with Him. Through her example she taught her six sons to love Jesus. Her 21 grandchildren and five great-grandchildren were also touched by her love for the Lord.

For as long as I can recall, Mother got up as early as four in the morning to read her Bible and pray. For hours she poured out her heart to her loving Father and found strength and encouragement in His Word. Then she woke up the rest of the family to say, "Time to pray!" Every morning we sat in a circle together, read our Bibles and prayed. I cannot remember a time that I did not see Mother during the morning hours with a Bible in her hands.

Clearly I remember the day she took me to a Gospel meeting. I was only eight years old, but that day I gave my heart to Jesus.

Committing my life to serve the Lord at age sixteen was a direct answer to my mother's prayers, too. For three and a half years she had fasted and prayed every Friday, asking the Lord to call one of her boys to become a missionary. And hardly a day went by that she herself did not visit several homes in my village to witness about the Lord.

I was on my way from India to South Korea to speak at a missions conference when she was admitted to the hospital with heart problems. I canceled my trip and stayed in India, visiting her daily, reading Bible verses and praying with her. As soon as I started reading a verse, she would finish it from memory. As she lay in her hospital bed she talked continually about Jesus.

The doctors, nurses and aides were all touched by her simple yet strong faith. "I am going home soon," she would tell them. "I am so happy."

The day before she died she took the hand of one of the young doctors who came to her bedside and told him, "You sit here and sing for me 'When the Roll Is Called Up Yonder I'll Be There.'"

The next morning my older brother phoned me to say that Mother had just passed away. She longed for her Father's house and had finally gone home.

After her death her doctors told me they had never seen such peace or assurance in a dying person.

Then came the funeral, the saddest day of my life. But thousands of people attended whose lives she had touched.

It was my responsibility as the youngest son to go to the coffin just before it was closed and cover my mother's face with a veil. My oldest brother sat at the foot of the coffin. As I lifted the veil, something struck me like lightning. I realized when I looked at her face that something was missing. It was her earring. I had never seen Mother without her earring. And the tiny gold chain that was the symbol of her marriage with my father—that was also missing from around her neck. And the ring on her finger that she always wore—it was gone, too.

There had been so much going on that I had not noticed these things until now, in the last few seconds that I would see her on this earth.

As I placed the veil over her face, one other thing stood out to me: Her Bible was not there.

After the coffin was closed, the crowd dispersed quietly and our family walked slowly home.

When we arrived home, my oldest brother, who now would handle our mother's affairs after her death, took me aside. Ever since our father had died in 1974, I had looked to him as the head of our family, as is the custom in my native land. I asked his opinion in matters pertaining to our family and respected his wishes.

"I know you have to go overseas soon," he said to me that afternoon. "But I thought you might like to know how much money Mother left in the bank."

I was curious. I imagined there would be a good sum of money, because we six children had given her quite a bit over the years.

"I looked through all her records," he told me, "and she has about two or three dollars left."

"What?" I was astounded.

"Yes," he replied. "And she also kept a record of what she did with her money."

We had never known what she did with it. But I discovered that afternoon that over the years she had been sending her money faithfully to dozens of missionaries, Bible school students and others who were serving the Lord.

"Oh, and by the way," my brother added, "she wanted her earring, her gold chain and her ring to be sold, and the money used for mission work among the unreached."

I was quiet after I heard this information. This was not just another great illustration of a saint of God; this was my mother. It hit close to home and made me think a lot about my own life and priorities.

In chapter 4 we talked about giving our lives to God as living sacrifices. In these next chapters I want to provide an eternal perspective on our material goods—and our families as well.

We cling to many things in this world, as Kuttapan did, the beggar who clung to his rupee coin. But we will not carry them with us.

How to Buy the Pearl

Jesus compared the Kingdom of heaven to "a merchant looking for fine pearls. When he found one of great value, he went away and sold everything he had and bought it" (Matthew 13:45–46).

Juan Carlos Ortiz, in his book *Call to Discipleship*, expands the story and gives us a better understanding of what absolute surrender—selling everything for the pearl—is all about.

> When a man finds Jesus, it costs him everything. Jesus has happiness, joy, peace, healing, security, eternity. Man marvels at such a pearl and says, "I want this pearl. How much does it cost?"
> The seller says, "It's too dear, too costly."
> "But how much?"
> "Well, it's very expensive."
> "Do you think I could buy it?"
> "Oh, of course. Anybody can."
> "But you say it's too expensive. How much is it?"
> "It costs everything you have—no more, no less—so anybody can buy it."
> "I'll buy it."
> "What do you have? Let's write it down."
> "I have $10,000 in the bank."
> "Good, $10,000. What else?"
> "I have nothing more. That's all I have."
> "Have you nothing more?"

"Well, I have some dollars here in my pocket."

"How many?"

"I'll see: thirty, forty, fifty, eighty, one hundred, one hundred twenty—one hundred twenty dollars."

"That's fine. What else do you have?"

"I have nothing else. That's all."

"Where do you live?"

"I live in my house."

"The house too."

"Then you mean I must live in the garage?"

"Have you a garage, too? That too. What else?"

"Do you mean that I must live in my car, then?"

"Have you a car?"

"I have two."

"Both become mine. Both cars. What else?"

"Well, you have the house, the garage, the cars, the money, everything."

"What else?"

"I have nothing else."

"Are you alone in the world?"

"No, I have a wife, two children. . . ."

"Your wife and children too."

"Too?"

"Yes, everything you have. What else?"

"I have nothing else, I am left alone now."

"Oh, you too. Everything. Everything becomes mine: wife, children, house, garage, cars, money, clothing, everything. And you too. Now you can use all those things here, but don't forget they are mine, as you are. When I need any of the things you are using, you must give them to me because now I am the owner."

What does it mean to give up everything for the pearl of great price?

The home of a close friend of mine has been broken into several times in the past few years. Most of the time, he told me, they found nothing worth stealing. The damage done to enter his home cost more than the theft itself.

"My main concern," he told me, "was not for the house but for my family. I was just glad they weren't at home when it happened. But after the last attempt I thought to myself, Why not put a note on the door saying, *Please come in— the door is unlocked. Take all you want.* There is really nothing to take!"

Then he laughed. "I found my imagination painting a picture of our house being dismantled by thieves or burning to the ground. And I was pleased and surprised by my reaction to the mental scenario. So what? I thought to myself. I'm not the owner; the Lord owns this house. Whether it's torn apart or burned to the ground—no problem. Where will we sleep tomorrow night? That's His problem."

Giving up everything for the pearl of great price means even more than relinquishing material things. It means relinquishing loved ones, too.

One day as I sat in an airport terminal waiting for a connecting flight, I prayed to the Lord and agonized over the many opportunities on the mission field. I thought particularly of the millions of Muslims throughout the world and the immense challenge before us to reach them with the Gospel.

Suddenly it was as if I were taken away to another time and place. A voice said, *Your son will finish high school and go to the mission field.*

As I looked I saw Daniel in Iran, going door to door and passing out Gospel tracts. Then I saw him being arrested. He was pushed blindfolded up against a wall. Shots rang out and he slumped over, blood pouring from a fatal wound to his head. I saw myself at home hearing the news for the first time, in shock.

Then the voice asked me, *Now what do you think?*

Back in the airport terminal, the question would not go away. What *did* I think? What would I do with my son?

From the very beginning Gisela and I have always told our children, "When you finish your studies, you can go to the mission field." Our children have always thought of their lives in terms of reaching the lost.

Now as I sat in the airport, I knew what my response would be. If Daniel went to Iran, distributed tracts door to door and was caught and killed, I could say only, "Praise the Lord. He did what God called him to do. He is not mine. My son belongs to the Lord."

What Will You Leave Behind?

Do I write these stories and scenarios just to impress you or to fill up pages in a book? No, I want to convey from these illustrations that your choice to live for Jesus is not just a means to escape hell. It is not just to have your sins forgiven or to have a nice, comfortable life here on earth with good fellowship and a free ride to heaven.

We saw in chapter 8 that life for Jesus is a battleground. Like it or not, we are in the enemy's territory. Jesus Himself was harassed continually by the powers of darkness and the enemies of the Gospel. He had no nice place to lay His head. He was misunderstood and rejected. He was often left alone, particularly at the hour of His greatest need. He died daily, and on the cross in great agony.

Paul and the other apostles followed in His footsteps.

Am I saying you are more spiritual if you walk around in rags and alienate yourself from society? No. And I do not want you to assume from what I am writing that giving up "rights" or comforts is all there is to life in Christ. Every truth in this world stretched beyond its limits will become a false doctrine. But when you commit yourself to live for Jesus, you cannot live just like everyone else. You must follow the Lord closely day by day. Only He can provide the balance you need. This is why we are told in the Word of

God that "those who are led by the Spirit of God are sons of God" (Romans 8:14).

As we walk through this life, we can choose to be led by the Spirit, or we can choose to be led by our own logic, by other people's opinions or by our own flesh. What led Mahatma Gandhi to live as he did, giving up everything to free India from colonial bondage? What led Gautama Buddha to walk away from his princely authority, his palace, his wife and child, and live as a monk for the rest of his life? It was not the Holy Spirit in either case. They themselves prompted their actions.

Our flesh will do a lot of good-looking things—a lot of praying, a lot of fasting, a lot of giving up. But the Word of God says, "If I give all I possess to the poor and surrender my body to the flames, but have not love, I gain nothing" (1 Corinthians 13:3).

If we are not controlled and led by love for God (as we saw in the story of the older brother in chapter 6), all the "right" outward behavior amounts to nothing. Since love is a fruit of the Holy Spirit, we must be filled continually with the Holy Spirit and led daily by Him.

"What is your life?" asks James 4:14. "You are a mist that appears for a little while and then vanishes."

Since your life is short, what will you leave behind?

My mother could not take her earring, her necklace, her ring, even her Bible, when she died. But the faith she instilled in the lives of her children, grandchildren and many others will live forever.

What will you leave behind? A few pieces of jewelry, a house, some cars, land, investments, money in the bank? Or will you leave more than that?

What about a son or daughter who is serving the Lord somewhere in the world? What about the memory that you lived for Jesus with all your heart—that you gave Him all you had and all you were to gain His Kingdom? What about the knowledge that you gave all you could to win the lost and dying souls of the world?

Jesus told His disciples the cost of the pearl of great price: "If anyone would come after me, he must deny himself and take up his cross and follow me" (Matthew 16:24). May you find the willingness in your heart to sell all you have for the pearl.

In the next chapter I want to show you how it was that Jesus paid the price. His eyes were not focused on the cross; He was looking beyond it.

Looking Beyond the Cross

Samuel lived a comfortable life in South India and made good money at his job. He was a believer who attended church faithfully, read his Bible and prayed. In 1984 when he attended a missions conference, he was challenged to give his life to serve the Lord full-time. There was no question in his mind that this was what Jesus wanted him to do. He went home, resigned his job and bought train tickets for himself and his family to the state of Karnataka. His was not a life he wanted to leave, but he was constrained by the love of the Lord.

Samuel chose one particular region in Karnataka because he had heard that this area was unreached. It was also notorious for being one of the most vicious anti-Gospel regions in the nation.

He managed to find a tiny hut they could call home and gradually learned the local language. As his language skills grew, he began to preach and witness in the community. One by one people came to know Jesus. A local church was established and Samuel was able to construct a small building where he and the believers met for worship.

Then came the day when Samuel led a Hindu priest to the Lord Jesus Christ. It is a daring act to win your local Hindu priest to the Lord in a community where the vast majority are Hindus. It is particularly risky when your area is a stronghold for a sect of fanatical, militant Hinduism. The goal of this sect: to make India a completely Hindu nation.

The news spread fast that the local temple priest was no longer the temple priest but was studying the Bible and sharing the Gospel. The priest's own brothers contacted the militant sect, specially trained to torture those who violate their religion or disobey orders.

The gang reacted swiftly to the news. One Sunday not long after, when Samuel had gathered the believers as usual for worship and teaching, a jeep pulled up in front of the building. A group of angry men walked into the church, right up to Samuel. They beat him viciously with iron rods, smashing his hand and breaking his arm, leg and collar bone.

Samuel's family and the other believers stood by helplessly, weeping at his terrible pain and the fact that they were unable to help him. Suddenly Samuel's seven-year-old son ran up to the front.

"Please don't kill our daddy!" he cried.

The gang leader turned on the little boy and swung his iron rod. The boy screamed in pain as the rod connected with his back and broke it. He fell to the dirt floor like a crumpled rag.

The gang members stepped back from their victims.

"This is only a warning to you to stop preaching this Jesus," they snarled. "Next time we come back, we won't leave you alive. We will kill you and bury you in this place."

They ran out the door, jumped into their jeep and drove off in a cloud of dust.

Samuel and his son were taken to a local hospital where they remained for several months.

A few months after this incident occurred, I was in India teaching at our local training center. I did not know that Samuel had also arrived there to meet with our leaders.

That evening during the prayer meeting, the Lord strongly impressed on my heart to pray for anyone who needed healing. So I said, "If anyone is sick tonight, no matter what it is, I want you to stand up. The Lord has promised us by His Word that He heals—and He will heal you tonight."

Several in the group stood up. As I prayed for each one, I knew the Lord would heal them.

The next day I found out Samuel had arrived. I asked him to share his testimony during the evening meeting. I knew it would be a challenge and encouragement to the young students at our training center who were planning themselves to go to the pioneer areas and witness for the Lord.

That evening when Samuel stood up, he added something to his testimony I had not expected.

"Last night before I came to your prayer meeting," he said, "I could not do anything with my hand." He held up the hand the Hindu gang had smashed. "I couldn't lift anything. I couldn't ride a bicycle. I couldn't even wring out a washcloth. But when Brother K. P. prayed last night, the Lord healed me! Now I can carry a bucket, I can move my hand any way I want and I can wring out my washcloth. The Lord has healed me!"

During those days I spent some time with Samuel. In the course of conversation I asked him, "What do you plan to do now?"

This young missionary looked at me with peaceful determination in his face. "I'm going back. Even if I'm killed, my blood will be the foundation for many more churches."

A few days later Samuel did go back, and he continues to share the Gospel in the same area of Karnataka. His little son is doing well and attends the local school. Samuel has baptized many more converts. And he has been beaten again.

This precious brother has counted the cost and is willing to pay the price. Why? Like Jesus, he is focusing on something else.

"I Looked for a Man among Them"

But before we see what that is, first tell me this: What would you do if you were in Samuel's place? If Hindu fanatics promised to come back and finish you off, would you keep preaching the Gospel?

I can tell you what I would want to do. I would look for a Bible verse to justify my getting out—a verse like, "At this, they picked up stones to stone him, but Jesus hid himself, slipping away from the temple grounds" (John 8:59). Or, "If anyone does not provide for his relatives, and especially for his immediate family, he has denied the faith and is worse than an unbeliever" (1 Timothy 5:8). *An unbeliever? My goodness, I'd better leave this place and take better care of my family. The Bible says so. Jesus left, too, you know!*

There must be hundreds of Bible verses I could isolate to justify my rational, sober-minded decision.

My best argument, of course, would be something like this: "I'm only forty-some years old. God wants me to use my brain for His Kingdom. With all the investment He's made in my life since I was sixteen, it wouldn't be right for me to be killed by some fanatics next week. I'm leaving this place so I'll have another forty years of my life to invest in God's Kingdom."

But what did Samuel say? "Even if I am killed, my blood will be the foundation for many more churches." So he went back—no arguments, no excuses, no rationalizations.

In Acts 20 when Paul was headed to Jerusalem, the Holy Spirit revealed to him, as He had revealed to him "in every city," that "prison and hardships" awaited him (verse 23). Imagine with me a scenario that might have taken place during that time.

Paul and the believers are in the middle of a prayer meeting when the Holy Spirit speaks through one of the believers: "This man Paul who is among you tonight will be bound and chained in Jerusalem. He will face afflictions and sufferings."

A shocked silence follows this prophecy. For these believers Paul is bigger than life. They love him. They are willing to die for him.

After the prayer meeting a group gathers around Paul.

One elder says, "Paul, you know the Holy Spirit spoke to you tonight."

"Yes," Paul replies, "I believe it *was* the Holy Spirit."

There is a collective sigh of relief among the group.

"So," the elder continues, "you won't be going to Jerusalem after all."

"Now that the Lord has warned you," adds another, "you can stay away from that city."

"I didn't say that," Paul tells them. "I only said I believe it's a word from the Lord. As a matter of fact, everywhere I've gone the Holy Spirit has said the same thing. But I'm still going to Jerusalem; I must."

The voices of the believers rise together in protest. "Paul, you *can't* go. Please! You're facing a threat to your life! Don't leave us. We need you."

"But I don't consider my own life dear to me," says Paul. "How can you kill a man who's already dead? I love my

Lord more than life itself, and there are many who still need to know Him."

Whether or not the conversations went exactly like this, the conflict was real—then and now. I have the firm conviction that God wants to do something wonderful in our generation with believers who are serious about following Him. He wants to reach every language, every tribe and every nation with the Gospel, and is still looking for those who will share His heart: "I looked for a man among them who would build up the wall and stand before me in the gap on behalf of the land so I would not have to destroy it, but I found none" (Ezekiel 22:30).

I believe right now He is building the foundation of that wall through us, His children.

Looking to Jesus

Recent studies of U.S. highways have shown a surprisingly high incidence of roadside collisions in which drivers collide with cars parked legally on the side of the road. Most of the drivers are not under the influence of alcohol or medication, and most of the collisions occur during favorable weather conditions.

As safety experts studied these statistics and determined to account for them, they came up with a fascinating explanation: the moth effect. Just as a moth is drawn to a flame, so a driver tends to steer his car involuntarily where he is focusing his eyes. Thus, if his eyes lock onto a vehicle parked by the side of the road rather than on the road in front of him, he may collide with that car.

We have to deal with the moth effect in our walk with the Lord. If we look back in our Christian life, or to the right or left, we will not only stop moving forward but will begin to head in the direction we are looking. But if we choose to obey and move forward in faith, looking at Jesus, we will find ourselves drawing closer to Him—and becoming more like Him in the process.

> Therefore . . . let us run with perseverance the race marked out for us. Let us fix our eyes on Jesus, the author and perfecter of our faith, who for the joy set before him endured the cross, scorning its shame, and sat down at the right hand of the throne of God. Consider him who endured such opposition from sinful men, so that you will not grow weary and lose heart.
>
> Hebrews 12:1–3

Here, then, is the secret that kept Jesus going: the joy beyond the cross. The secret that kept Paul going, and the one that keeps Samuel going, is the joy of looking to Jesus. The Lord may ask us to do something that opposes every grain of logic within us. Our emotions may rise up in protest against it. Those around us may do their best to convince us to look back. The *only* way we will have the strength to do what God asks us to do is by keeping our eyes on Jesus!

The Christian life, according to the author of Hebrews, is like running a race. We have laid aside "everything that hinders and the sin that so easily entangles" (Hebrews 12:1). We have come to the point where we are willing to break from the past and begin a new life in Jesus. As we start our race, we face hardships and distractions. Our enemy knows our weaknesses and tries his best to put us out of the race.

But as we begin the course and strain our eyes down the track toward the finish line, we see Someone familiar: It is Jesus! He has finished His race and is waiting for us. If He has already completed the race, so can we! As we focus our eyes on Him, all the sounds and sights that distract us from the race fade away. We can even forget our weariness as we run steadily down the track, our eyes fixed on Jesus only.

Our race is not yet completed, of course. We face daily, hourly, minute-by-minute choices to keep looking forward. We can be sure there will continue to be difficulties and distractions. Sometimes we stumble and fall and have to repent of our sins. But we can be sure Jesus will be waiting for us at the finish line.

Paul told the Philippians that he knew he had not arrived spiritually.

> But one thing I do: Forgetting what is behind and straining toward what is ahead, I press on toward the goal to win the prize for which God has called me heavenward in Christ Jesus.
>
> Philippians 3:13–14

This is the secret to accepting the cross, to paying the price no matter how great, no matter what others say. Jesus endured the cross, the pain, the agony, the shame and the suffering, "for the joy set before him." He looked beyond the cross and saw the joy that was waiting. This is what enabled Him to endure the horrible suffering and death He experienced for us.

What will it take for you to be able to pick up your cross daily and follow Jesus? How can you possibly pay the price that is required of you? You can do it only as you look beyond the cross and see the joy that is set before you— joy that is indescribable and glorious, joy that will make every ounce of suffering and inconvenience worth it all.

I do not know where you are in your spiritual life, but I pray that the enemy will not steal away your affection from the One who has paid with His blood to redeem you. I pray that you will not walk away from Him. I pray that you will be willing to pay the price in order to follow Jesus.

It is for those more than two billion souls who have not heard the Gospel that we must live. It is for them that we must give up the comfortable life this world offers us. For them we must be willing to live a life that people misunderstand; willing to walk away from all that we could accumulate on this earth and be content with what the Lord gives us. While you are on this earth, make it your life's ambition to take as many souls as possible with you to heaven.

God will give you the grace to live this life as He calls you. In the light of eternity, the battle is really not that long. I pray that you will look beyond the cross, beyond the pain and sacrifice, and see Jesus waiting there for you. The joy that awaits you is far greater than any price you have to pay.

Just a Handful of Dust

I stood up in my hotel room and hung up the phone—hard. I had just talked with our headquarters in India, and what I had heard outraged me. I wanted to do something about it, but there was nothing I could do until I got to India on my next trip. I sat down on the bed and stewed about the information I had just received.

Moses Paulose, one of our most respected native missionary leaders, has a ministry on the Hindu pilgrimage island of Rameswaram, off the southeastern tip of India. Each year millions of devout Hindus flock to the island in hopes that their sins will be forgiven when they bathe in what they consider the sacred waters of the Indian Ocean. Paulose and his team are able to reach out to people from nearly every language group on the Indian subcontinent.

Several months before, we had arranged for Paulose to take a group of young people from several Bible schools for a summer of practical training. I knew that if anyone could teach those students the meaning of discipleship, it would be Paulose.

But one young man from my own village had been with Paulose. When I saw him I was shocked. Normally I would consider him skinny anyway, but after his time in Rameswaram he looked as if he had lost half his weight!

And now I had learned that by the end of the first month, more than seventy percent of these young people had left! One day when Paulose had arrived home, he had apparently discovered that the last of the deserters had sneaked out, bought a train ticket with some borrowed money and taken off. Only one or two ended up staying for the entire summer.

So I was angry. We had invested time, energy and our reputation to send these Bible school students for training. We had sent money to Paulose for their food and other necessities. Why on earth was he treating them so badly? And why did he let them out of the battle? These looked like lost opportunities to me.

I resolved to confront Paulose the next time I saw him.

Sure enough, the next time I traveled to India I met Paulose the very first week. Without even asking how his ministry was going, I jumped on him, venting my frustrations about this failed ministry opportunity and his manner of training these students. On and on I went, accusing him—justly, I felt—of what seemed to be poor judgment.

Moses Paulose wears a perpetual smile on his face. If you have something to say, he listens until you are through. Then, calmly and quietly, he speaks just a few sentences. When he is finished, you do not know what else to say.

Now, in his quiet way, Paulose said simply, "Do you know that when seventy people come with me for training, I realize even before they arrive that only a handful will make it?"

"What are you talking about?" I asked, incredulous.

"You know very well that most Bible colleges and seminaries do not teach students to be Christlike disciples. When they come to me for training, I do not ask them to do things I don't do. Everywhere they go, I go with them. I design everything to make them count the cost. I do not want to spend three months just to find out that they will not make it. So right from the start I give them the chance to count the cost. Most of them go back.

"K. P.," he finished with his little smile, "this is not the first time this has happened. You've only just now come to learn what has been happening here."

Needless to say, I was silent. There was nothing more to say. Nor could I say anything to change what Paulose was doing. But I determined to keep my eye on his ministry.

Rameswaram was one of the places where hundreds of thousands of refugees arrived during the civil war in Sri Lanka. Haggard and half-dead from lack of food, they had barely escaped with their lives. Each morning Paulose and his team of more than twenty believers rose early to go to the seashore and count the number of refugees who had come in. Then they went back to cook breakfast and prepare tea for these people. Every day was full of ministry and outreach in Rameswaram and the surrounding villages.

I do not know how many hours of sleep the team members got during those days of ministering to the refugees. But Paulose and his team labored seven days a week for months on end.

One of the team members who worked alongside Paulose came from a middle-class family. His family was upset with him, I learned, because he chose not to marry. Once again I questioned Paulose.

"Is this because you are brainwashing him with your radical way of living?" I asked.

"I would be happy for him to get married," Paulose replied. "I would gladly help in any way. I'm married and have six children of my own. Why don't you talk to him?"

So I did. The next time I saw the young man, I asked, "Is everything all right with you?"

"Yes, fine," he replied.

"What about your plans to get married?" I probed.

"I want to be able to serve the Lord without being married."

I thought if I waited until the next time I saw him, he might be willing for me to help him find a wife. (That's how we do it in India.) But each time I asked, the young man told me firmly no.

Then it began to dawn on me how Paulose could build a team of people willing to live a grueling lifestyle and minister the Gospel under very difficult circumstances. He did not draw these team members by compulsion or force. Rather, as he said, he gave them the chance to count the cost. A few, like him, were willing to die for the sake of the cross. Having counted the cost, they loved Jesus more than life itself.

Standing on Emptiness

I am sure that Paulose's call from the Lord is unique, just as the apostle Paul's was. But I want you to think seriously about what you have just read and what you are about to read.

From my conversations with Paulose, I recognized a basic principle involving our walk with the Lord and our service to Him: *God wants us, in our life and ministry for Him, to stand on emptiness.*

What is emptiness? It is a void, a vacuum, total nothingness. It is like holding onto something you cannot tangibly feel. Your eyes see nothing but still you follow. Your feet step out onto what looks like thin air. Standing on emptiness means we are stripped of not only tangible things but intangible as well. Everything we are, everything we trust—our own know-how, abilities, talents, strength—all are gone. Nothing we do for the Lord can ever come from our own resources.

Many people around the world strip themselves of material goods in order to seek internal peace. In India more than any other country, thousands teach and practice asceticism after the example of Buddha, the wealthy prince who left his wife and child and wandered around the country for the rest of his life meditating.

But this is not what I mean by standing on emptiness. What Buddha did, and what many do today, is only the attempt of the self to gain salvation. In biblical terms, the Lord wants us to come to a place where we are drawing on nothing but Him so that, as Paul said, "this all-surpassing power is from God and not from us" (2 Corinthians 4:7). There is no way we can say, "I did that."

Jesus told the crowds, "If anyone comes to me and does not hate his father and mother, his wife and children, his brothers and sisters—yes, even his own life—he cannot be my disciple" (Luke 14:26).

Then there was the rich young ruler who lacked only one thing to inherit eternal life. Jesus told him, "Sell everything you have and give to the poor, and you will have treasure in heaven. Then come, follow me" (Luke 18:22). The young man went away troubled because he loved his riches more than he did eternal life.

Throughout the Bible we see God drawing His people to a place where they were suspended over empty space, where they were challenged to operate out of faith and total dependence, where there was nothing tangible to cling to but Him. Let's take a quick trip through the Old and New Testaments and look at nine examples—and nine possible excuses for *not* standing on emptiness.

"It's Physically Impossible"

God promised Abraham from the very beginning that He would produce from him a great nation, but He waited to fulfill that promise until it seemed impossible to Abraham.

Finally Abraham came to the place where he could say, "Just look at me, Lord. I'm a wrinkled old man. There's nothing left in my body that could produce a child. It's as good as dead. And look at Sarah—she's an old woman. Her ability to bear children ceased long ago. I'm a hundred, Lord, and she's ninety—and You still say we're going to have a child!"

God waited until Abraham had nothing humanly speaking to hold onto; he was totally dependent on God for the fulfillment of the promise. Abraham and Sarah knew that if they were still to have a child, it would have to be an act of God.

Then God was able to work (see Genesis 21).

"We Have an Agenda"

Some centuries later, when God led the children of Israel out of Egypt, He miraculously spared their oldest sons from the final plague. He opened the Red Sea for them to walk through on dry ground. He provided food and water for them each step of the way.

But what happened in the camp? They grumbled because God did not deliver according to their schedule. They had an agenda, perhaps something like this: "Tomorrow we'll have breakfast, lunch and dinner at these set times. The first night we'll have beef, the next night chicken and the next night fish. When we reach that certain spot, we'll have water. And after three months we'll need a change of clothing and shoes."

Reasonable expectations, but that is not how God led them. "Whenever the cloud lifted from above the tabernacle, they would set out; but if the cloud did not lift, they did not set out—until the day it lifted" (Exodus 40:36–37).

What was God trying to do? He wanted them to focus their hearts not on what they would eat the next day, or on where they would go, but on Him.

"We Need All the Help We Can Get"

Gideon had 32,000 warriors with him when God first led him to war against the Midianites. But God told him, "You have too many men for me to deliver Midian into their hands" (Judges 7:2). So the Lord reduced the number of the army to ten thousand.

Gideon must have been thinking, *Too many men? The army of the Midianites is without number—like grasshoppers camped out there in the valley. We need all the people we can get!*

Then the Lord reduced the number further. He told Gideon to choose only the men who, drinking from the water, lapped from their hands to their mouths and did not put their mouths directly to the water. Only three hundred drank in this way.

What was God's purpose in this selection process? To show that it would be His victory alone, and to weed out those who did not put their trust wholly in the Lord. The remaining three hundred men were not stupid; they knew the enemy they were about to fight, and that it was impossible, from a human standpoint, to win. Yet they were willing to go into battle regardless of the outcome because they realized the victory did not depend on them. They were willing to stand on emptiness. God would fight for them.

"We Want Someone More Predictable"

Do you remember when Israel clamored for a king? They told Samuel, "Appoint a king to lead us, such as all the other nations have" (1 Samuel 8:5).

Have you ever wondered why these people longed for someone to rule over them? They wanted to be sure what would happen tomorrow. They wanted to be confident that things would work out a certain way. They wanted that secure feeling of knowing that the storehouses were full and that if something disastrous happened, a king would be there to take care of them and defend them with his army.

Humanly speaking their request made sense. But God wanted them to come to a place where they were standing on emptiness, where they would say, "We don't know about tomorrow, but the Lord is our tomorrow. He is all we need." So God told the prophet Samuel, "It is not you they have rejected as their king, but me" (see verse 7).

Samuel went back and warned the people how a king would oppress them. A king would take their sons and daughters, fields and vineyards, donkeys and sheep, and themselves to be his servants.

But the Israelites wanted a king. God was so unpredictable! They failed Him and He walked away. They went to fight and many were killed. Later He told them it happened because they sinned and that they had better repent. Couldn't He help them out when they were in a tight spot and tell them *later* about their sins? No, they wanted an earthly king.

The Israelites were no different from us. And in the end, of course, God gave them what they wanted.

"There's Strength in Numbers"

Move forward through the years to when Israel's second king, David, commanded his captain to take a census of the army of Israel. Joab and the army commanders protested: God was the One who had given David the fighting men; it did not matter how many there were.

But "the king's word . . . overruled Joab" (2 Samuel 24:4) and seventy thousand Israelites were wiped out as a result of David's disobedience to God.

This does not seem reasonable to us. After all, David was the king. Didn't he have every right to know what he had in terms of strength, just in case another army rose up against Israel? Isn't it logical to take inventory?

But even before God's judgment, David knew he had sinned. He had forgotten the times when he was a young boy watching the sheep and had to face wild animals; the time he had confronted Goliath. Who had given David these victories? All he had had to count on then was God. God was all he needed.

The problem in this story was David's inner attitude. He had come to a place in his life where he no longer wanted to stand on emptiness; he wanted certainty and knowledge. And his pride led to immediate, terrible destruction.

"Look What I've Accomplished"

Uzziah, who began his reign at the age of sixteen, was one of the kings of Judah who followed the Lord. We learn from 2 Chronicles 26 that Uzziah accomplished an incredible number of tasks while he was king: "He did what was right in the eyes of the LORD. . . . As long as he sought the LORD, God gave him success" (verses 4–5). Verse 7 adds, "God helped him." Remember, we are talking about a sixteen-year-old boy!

But Uzziah's life did not end as well as it had begun. "After Uzziah became powerful, his pride led to his downfall" (verse 16). He was no longer an unsure, awkward adolescent. Now he knew his way around. He had a reputation. He could negotiate and wheel and deal. Uzziah was a self-made man. He knew the correct protocol for every situation and had an air of dignity about him.

Do you see what can happen when you trust in your own strength? Your heart becomes lifted up to your own destruction. The attitude of the heart for which we must continually be on guard is the attitude when we think we have it made.

"Is There Something Else We Can Cling To?"

The story of Job offers a fascinating contrast. In order to prove that Job was not righteous and godly but would curse God to His face, Satan stripped him of everything—house, land, herds, children. Finally Job found himself on a heap of ashes, his body covered with boils, scraping himself with a piece of pottery.

At least I have my wife to stand by me, Job might have said to himself. *She's lived with me for many years, slept with me, borne my children. She knows my thoughts, sees my life. She'll understand.*

But his wife turned to him and said, "Why are you suffering like this? Curse God so you can at least die and get out of your misery."

Well, I have my friends to support me, Job may have thought. *Even if all is lost, even if I'm sick for many years to come, they're here. They can't heal me or do anything to change my situation, but at least they understand me and can offer some inner courage to help me through these struggles.*

But his friends spent nearly the rest of the book misunderstanding and accusing him. He could hardly open his mouth before they used what he said against him.

Everything Job had was gone. He was left with nothing to stand on. But that was all right; he recognized something more real than everything else. In the middle of it all, despite the accusations mounted against him, Job said, "I know that my Redeemer lives" (Job 19:25).

In the end Job came through the test, pure and approved.

"Is There Someone Else We Can Turn To?"

Some think Jesus had only twelve disciples, but we read in the Gospels that He had many more than that. At one point in His ministry, at least 82 men followed Jesus.

Everything was going wonderfully for them. They were fed and taken care of, thousands were coming to see Jesus and spectacular miracles were being performed. It was a great life!

Then one day Jesus began to tell them the other side of the story. He told them that He was going to die.

This was new information for them. He explained more about His suffering and coming death on the cross by telling them that He must give them His body and blood in order for them to have life. On hearing this, many of his disciples just walked away. In the end, only a few remained.

"You do not want to leave too, do you?" Jesus asked the Twelve.

Simon Peter answered him, "Lord, to whom shall we go? You have the words of eternal life."

John 6:67–68

Most saw the cross as a means of loss, discouragement and death. Only a few saw the life and hope that the cross had to offer.

Walking with Jesus is always like this. A huge crowd may start out, just as in a marathon, but only a few make it to the end.

"What about My Rights?"

Jesus told a parable of a servant who worked all day in the fields, plowing and watching the sheep. At the end of the day, when his master arrived home, the servant prepared his supper and waited on him while he ate. Afterward the servant cleaned up. And not until late into the evening did the servant sit down to eat his own supper.

What does Jesus say this servant's response—and ours—should be? "We are unworthy servants; we have only done our duty" (Luke 17:10).

This is exactly where the Lord wants us to be. After all we have done, we are still unworthy servants. Nothing I am and nothing I have done gives me even one square inch to stand on and say, "I've done a good job. I deserve some commendation."

As the lines in the familiar hymn "Rock of Ages" put it,

> Nothing in my hand I bring,
> Simply to Thy cross I cling.

The Lesson of the Dollar Bills

Clinging only to God and nothing else is a lesson I have to keep remembering.

Not too long ago Margaret, our bookkeeper for our Texas office, brought me an envelope and showed me what was inside. Four dollar bills—very special ones. I had written on each of them in red and given them to her to keep, but I had forgotten they were there.

A few years before, Gisela and I had sat at our dinner table with Terry, another member of our staff, and reminisced about the years we each had spent with Operation Mobilization. We remembered "the good old days" when we walked from village to village, and how our ministry had changed dramatically when we were able to use a truck or van to get from place to place. Then we had been able to move out full steam ahead to penetrate unreached areas with the Gospel.

How wonderful it would be, we thought now around the dining room table, to purchase vehicles for our native missionaries! We could equip them with Gospel literature, a generator, a projector and an Indian-made film on the life of Christ. Then we could send teams to remote areas to spread the Gospel.

Purchasing and equipping even one van was an ordeal. At $12,000 each, we did not come by them easily. But the more we talked, the more convinced we became that van teams could be a major force in reaching pioneer areas for Christ.

As we sat at the table, I took a dollar bill from my wallet and wrote on it in big red letters, "The first dollar down payment, by faith, toward the purchase of 100 vehicles." I took another dollar bill and wrote, "The first dollar down payment toward the purchase of 100 projectors." In a few moments four bills sat on the table representing our faith in the Lord to provide for this goal.

To date we have received enough funds to purchase more than 84 vans and equip them to reach pioneer areas that have never had a Gospel witness! This means that on each van team, five missionaries can travel all over India, going to thousands of villages and sharing the love of Jesus. This is the first time the majority of these simple village people have ever heard the name of Jesus.

So when Margaret showed me those four dollar bills in the envelope, I was reminded that nothing we had done had made this come to pass. It was God and God alone who did it.

Whenever I remember David's prayer in Psalm 19, my heart is sobered: "Keep back thy servant also from presumptuous sins; let them not have dominion over me" (Psalm 19:13 KJV). We must not take the goodness of the Lord for granted or indulge the slightest sense of pride or self-congratulation. And we must never entertain thoughts like, *Based on my past actions, I have it made* or *We can do it ourselves—all we need is some ingenious planning.*

Where we have strengths that God can use, let us say honestly to Him, "I acknowledge that I am strong in these areas, but they are gifts from You, and I surrender them to You to use as You see fit." Nothing we do for the Lord ever comes from our own resources.

Our opportunities are unlimited. But beyond the challenge to spread the Gospel into developing nations, something else is far more pressing: *We are totally dependent on God.* If we do not look to Him but rather to ourselves to meet our needs, only disaster can result.

Something wonderful happens, on the other hand, when we regard ourselves as helplessly dependent on the Lord. In our hearts and attitudes, we must remain as children before Him. If we are enabled to accomplish anything, it is because of the Lord and His grace. The secret of His blessing on any work, large or small, is that all the glory goes to Him.

Serving Our Generation

But we are self-willed individuals who live in flesh-and-blood bodies and strive naturally for personal praise. How can we regard ourselves as helplessly dependent on the Lord and give Him all the glory? Look at Psalm 103:14: "He knows how we are formed, he remembers that we are dust." This verse assures me that the Lord knows the stuff I am made of. The question is, Am I able to remember it? *Will I daily recognize that all I am made of is a little handful of dust?*

The Lord rescues us repeatedly from our tendency to stop depending on Him and start depending on ourselves. He often keeps us from doing things in our own flesh instead of in His strength. Sometimes, in His mercy, He even causes those things to fail.

Because when all is said and done, when history is sealed up and time runs out, God will make sure that nothing that is a product of the flesh will last for eternity. He has never accepted a work of our flesh and He never will, however good it might look to us. Nothing, not preaching thousands of sermons, not even seeming to turn the world upside-down, will enter eternity if it has been a product of our flesh. Anything lasting for eternity will have been done by Him and Him alone.

We must heed the warning of God to the children of Israel as they were about to pass over the Jordan River into the Promised Land:

> When you have eaten and are satisfied, praise the LORD your God for the good land he has given you. . . . Otherwise, when you eat and are satisfied, when you build fine houses and settle down, and when your herds and flocks grow large and your silver and gold increase and all you have is multiplied, then your heart will become proud and you will forget the LORD your God. . . . You may say to yourself, "My power and the strength of my hands have produced this wealth for me."
>
> Deuteronomy 8:10, 12–14, 17

We are no different than the children of Israel. Take a look around you at the people and ministries you know God has called to do His heart's desire. Often flesh gets in the way. People become arrogant and take the glory for themselves. When the Lord uses people for His purposes, He often has to strip away dependence on intelligence, education, abilities, strengths. He has to make them nothing before He can build them back up again for His service.

It is refreshing to see how God carries along a person or ministry that acknowledges dependence on Him. Some things we plan never take place. Other things we never expect may happen in a mighty way. This helps us know beyond a shadow of a doubt that God has accomplished these things.

We read this about a great man of God: "When David had served God's purpose in his own generation, he fell asleep" (Acts 13:36). After doing all the things we know we should do, we have not gained any credit. It is God's purpose and in His strength that we are serving.

I pray that we will no longer trust our own resources or understanding. Whatever God has called you to do, you can accomplish it when the Lord is doing it and not you. He is looking not for Bible knowledge, impeccable theology, great zeal, missions conferences or computer information networks. He is looking for surrender—men and women at home who are willing to say, "My life no longer belongs to me; I have given it as a sacrifice." He is looking for men and women on the mission field who are willing to say, "I came to this place with a one-way ticket. They can kill me if they want, but I am here to preach the Gospel."

How can we be sure we will be able to accomplish the task of world evangelism? Can we handle the work? Isn't the plan to evangelize the world a little ambitious?

All I can say is that the Lord is with us. Have you seen how the wind comes and carries off the dry leaves from beneath a tree? That is the best way for me to explain what I mean. Let the wind of God blow you away and carry you wherever He wishes.

And then what? Don't we need to know more than that?

No. I do not know where the Lord will have you or me go tomorrow or next year. All I know is that I am standing on emptiness and declaring total dependence on the Lord. I am but a handful of dust. I have nothing in myself that I can cling to, no strength of my own to carry me. It is He who leads me, whether that means having everything or having nothing. All that matters is Him.

Stripping Away Our Secret Longings

I was sitting at my desk working on correspondence and phone contacts when a knock came at the door.

"Come in," I called.

Dave, our computer department manager, poked his head in the door. "I have some information here I think you'd like to see."

We were in the process of making a decision on a much-needed computer system for our headquarters in Texas. As I read through Dave's figures and dates that plotted our growth in the near future, I found myself getting excited.

Wow! I thought. *This is fantastic! We're doing really well.*

My mind started to project into the next five to ten years, until it seemed to me that we were going to become one of the important ministries in the days to come.

But as soon as Dave left, the Lord began to speak to my heart: *What is this ministry really all about? Are these plans what you are setting your hopes on? Are you standing on your own dreams and schemes?*

I had done it again. Not only had I forgotten for a few moments that it was the Lord who had brought us to the place we were today, but I had been longing secretly for more acceptance, more recognition. I had to repent of these longings and think back to where I had come from.

I joined Operation Mobilization in 1966 and began eight years of intensive Gospel outreach. I came as a sixteen-year-old boy, skinny legs poking out through my shorts, still barefoot and knowing no language other than my native tongue. I did not know much about anything, but I was certain of God's calling on my life.

Each year the leadership of OM India gathered the entire force of missionaries together—between three and four hundred of us—for a conference. New strategies were planned and we were challenged, refreshed and encouraged.

Typically one of the leaders stood up in front of us and said, "Brothers and sisters, we need to pray—we have no more food."

I was hungry, so I prayed! It was wonderful to see how the Lord answered our prayers, meeting all our needs.

After the conference we were divided into teams of eight or nine members. Each team was assigned an area of India. We had a leader and an old, beat-up truck to carry literature. We were given a few dollars for food, our truck was filled with tracts and Gospel literature, and off we went, sitting on crates in the back of the truck as it swerved and bounced over thousands of miles of Indian roads.

We would drive as far as we could until the truck ran out of diesel. By that time our money had run out as well. Our leader would say, "Let's pray; then we'll go and sell our Gospel literature." By the afternoon we would have enough money from the sale of our literature to buy a few *chappatis* (tortilla-like breads) for each of us, as well as fill the truck with more diesel.

"All right," our leader would say, "one hour of rest, then we'll be going again."

Day in and day out, that is how we lived.

Some of the local churches would not receive our teams because they perceived us to be fanatics. "These OM people make us feel as though we're going to hell," they would say. "We don't want their preaching."

So we would sleep on the side of the road under the truck. One night it rained so hard that even the roadside was filled with a swirling, muddy flood. Shivering like wet rats, our clothes plastered to our skin, we all crawled into the back of the truck, where we hardly found even a place to sit. Bright and early the next morning we moved on.

Several years went by, and I became a team leader. One day in North India I was called on to preach in a meeting. At that point in my life I owned two shirts, two pairs of pants and a pair of sneakers. But North India in the wintertime is a very cold place, and today was no exception.

The electricity had gone out, so all the windows were open for light. The winter wind blew mercilessly through the building. I was freezing. As I stood there in my thin shirt, holding my Bible, everyone waited expectantly. They were all wearing thick woolen blankets and coats. I shivered. My knees were knocking together and my teeth were chattering so hard I could no longer speak.

Lord, I said in my heart, *I believe I am doing what You told me to do, but I can't even open my mouth, much less talk. I want to talk to these people about You, but I can't. Please help me.*

Suddenly I felt as if there were a wall of fire around me. Instantly I was warm! The Lord had answered my prayer.

That day I preached on hell, and a few were saved at the end of my message. But I was warm only during the time I preached! As soon as I finished I began to shiver and chatter once again.

All the years I was with this Gospel team, we lived out some of the passages in the New Testament. We were faced continually with loss, persecution, beatings and stonings, but we never worried whether we would live or die. We had just one thought in our hearts: *These people don't know the Lord. Live or die—fine. We will preach the Gospel. If we are killed, praise the Lord—heaven is a better place anyway.*

"I Consider Them Rubbish"

In the last chapter we said that it is by God's strength alone that we accomplish anything for Him. In this chapter we examine a corresponding truth: it must be God's agenda alone that guides us. As committed, sober-minded believers, we must identify and strip away any secret longings that we find within ourselves for acceptance, security, reputation, advancement, the approval of others, anything that is not from God. I can tell you from personal experience, it is dangerous to fall into this trap!

Just before Moses' death, God called him to present himself, along with Joshua, in the Tabernacle. There He gave Moses a solemn look at the future:

> "You are going to rest with your fathers, and these people will soon prostitute themselves to the foreign gods of the land they are entering. They will forsake me and break the covenant I made with them. On that day I will become angry with them and forsake them; I will hide my face from them, and they will be destroyed."
>
> Deuteronomy 31:16–17

To avoid the same idolatry, we must look prayerfully to the Lord and continuously offer up any secret longings of our hearts. Are you worshiping any foreign gods? Make it a practice to keep surrendering to God your future, your plans, your ideas, your dreams, your hopes. Give Him the freedom to lead you wherever He chooses.

Jesus laid down His own desires when He was led outside of the city gate bearing the shame of the cross. We are called to follow Him: "Let us, then, go to him outside the camp, bearing the disgrace he bore" (Hebrews 13:13). I am not saying you have to endure nakedness or crucifixion to prove your spirituality. But I cannot emphasize too strongly how vital it is to come to the place where you relinquish every longing in your heart to the Lord.

The apostle Paul did. He was obviously an intelligent man. He presents his résumé to us in Philippians 3: He was well-educated and, "as for legalistic righteousness, fault-less" (verse 6). But he goes on to say,

> Whatever was to my profit I now consider loss for the sake of Christ. What is more, I consider everything a loss com-pared to the surpassing greatness of knowing Christ Jesus my Lord, for whose sake I have lost all things. I consider them rubbish, that I may gain Christ and be found in him, not having a righteousness of my own. . . .
>
> verses 7–9

All the things we would consider benefits—background, intelligence, abilities, education, influence—Paul counted as dung. Trash. Rubbish. Toward the end of his life, when he knew his enemies were waiting for him, he said, "I consider my life worth nothing to me, if only I may finish the race and complete the task the Lord Jesus has given me—the task of testifying to the gospel of God's grace" (Acts 20:24).

Paul did not cling to his life. There was nothing he stood on that he was afraid of falling from, no ambition he was clinging to that he was afraid of losing. He cherished only "the task the Lord Jesus has given me."

Plans and strategies are not wrong, but we must commit ourselves only to the task He has given us and cast every-thing else aside.

Willing to Die

While I was on a past trip to India, a letter arrived for me. Since it was certified, I had to sign for it. I opened the envelope and found a letter wrapped around several pages from a Bible. The portions were half-burned and the edges charred. A little ash remained in the envelope. As I unfolded the letter and began to read it, I sat down slowly. The letter was from one of the leaders of a militant Hindu movement. It described all the things I was involved in—missionary support, prayer meetings, a radio program, everything. The list was intended to convince me that I was being watched closely.

"We are sending you this letter as a warning," the leader wrote. "Unless you stop these activities, you will not be alive many more days or months."

He had signed his letter in blood.

This letter made me think.

What are we about in this ministry? I asked myself. *What are we creating on the mission field? What kind of workers and leaders are we producing? What direction are we heading? What kind of life are we challenging people to live?*

And I think about Isaac.

Before he was saved, Isaac was a devout Hindu. To please his gods, he would spend a month or two preparing himself for a special ceremony. During this time he would avoid certain foods, according to the likes or dislikes of the demon gods he worshiped, who would then come to possess Isaac's body. Isaac offered the blood of nearly sixty chickens to these deities. As the time drew near, he would sit and chant while beating a drum. When he went into a trance, the ceremony began. Because of the power of the demons that possessed him, Isaac was able to pierce his cheeks with arrows, walk on fire and put hooks through the muscles of his back to pull an idol on a cart.

When Isaac found Jesus, he forsook his gods and was delivered from all demonic possession. Now he travels to different areas as an evangelist, sharing the Gospel and winning souls to Jesus.

But not without a price.

A short while ago Isaac went to a nearby village to preach and share his testimony. While he was speaking, a gang grabbed him and told him, "Just as you used to cut the chickens' throats and shed their blood, now we will cut you and shed *your* blood!"

They dragged him from the village to a heavily wooded area and beat him severely. Then they tied him to a tree, pulling his hands backwards around the trunk, and left to call more people to kill him. They had selected the tree carefully: It was covered with fierce biting ants.

The ants crawled all over his body, biting him repeatedly. Isaac was in terrible pain and lapsed in and out of consciousness.

Then, in the haze of his agony, he saw an old woman, perhaps eighty years old, standing in front of him. Untying him she said, "You must leave here quickly."

He did as he was told. But as he hurried off before his persecutors returned, he looked back for the old lady. She had vanished. Then Isaac realized God had provided a way for his escape.

Just a week later Isaac came to a local pastors' conference and shared his testimony. The pastors were challenged and encouraged to hear of his faith in the Lord and his willingness to lay down his life.

So as I thought about the letter from the Hindu fanatic and about Isaac's singlehearted commitment, the Lord impressed me that it was *His* task I was about. Part of this task is leaving behind my own ambitions for the ministry, my own desires to be accepted, and follow the Lord's agenda completely—just like the skinny kid in shorts who aspired to do nothing but stand and preach the Gospel to people who had never heard.

More like Jesus

How about you? Have you stripped yourself of the secret longings deep within your heart for acceptance, security and recognition? Is there something the Lord has asked you to do that you have put off because you are afraid you will lose control of the situation? Is your prayer life proof of your total dependence on the Lord? Do you ask Him to show you His plans or are you asking Him, in effect, to bless your own agenda? Can you honestly say that this world is not your home and that you are simply passing through?

If someone were to point a gun at you and say, "Deny Christ or I'll kill you," what would your response be? Would you say, as Paul did, "I consider my life worth nothing to me"? What has hindered you from giving unselfishly to reach the lost in our generation?

The days before us will not be easy ones—either for our brothers and sisters on the mission field or for believers in the West. I foresee major attacks, opposition, even martyrdom for many of our missionaries. And in a country like India, I foresee that sometime in the near future many thousands will be killed for their faith. All the signs point to this.

What does it take to live in times like these?

It takes believers who have nothing but God to cling to, because if there were something left in their lives that they counted dear, they would run off in fear.

No one can write any words that will make us something we are not. I can share examples and illustrations, but God has to do the work within us, developing our hearts and our attitudes.

The most vital thing for all of us, as we grow in our walks with the Lord and answer the call of eternity, is to become more like Jesus.

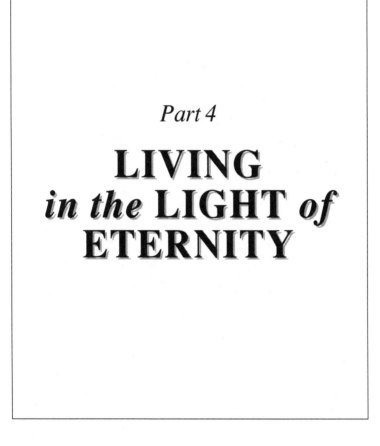

Part 4

LIVING
in the LIGHT *of*
ETERNITY

Giving Our Children the Best We Know

Nearly forty years ago an elderly Christian woman in Wyckoff, New Jersey, began a lonely eighteen-year prayer vigil. She lived near a busy high school and often watched the teenagers come and go. One of the most difficult boys, she knew from her observations, was a kid named George. Dorothea Clapp began to pray daily for his conversion. Then she sent him a copy of the Gospel of John.

Two years later he received Christ as his Savior.

As he began to grow as a Christian, Mrs. Clapp prayed for his spiritual development and talked with him. Then George began to witness to his classmates. Over 125 came to Christ as a result! Later as a college student, George made trips into Mexico with a group of friends who shared his heart for the lost.

Gradually the Lord expanded the vision of these young people to include nearly sixty other countries. Eventually their zeal led others to fan out across the world and start youth mission movements in many nations. One of the witnessing teams came to India and visited my village when I was sixteen—the barefoot boy unable to read or write English. The team challenged me to take the Gospel north to the lost millions of Rajasthan, the Punjab and the Himalayas.

Today, as a result of the vision the Lord placed in my heart during that time, Gospel for Asia is able to sponsor thousands of full-time missionaries in eleven Asian nations. And mine is only one of many lives that have been touched.

The young man's name, of course, was George Verwer. As a result of Mrs. Clapp's prayer and interest in his salvation, millions have heard the Gospel through Operation Mobilization. And out of OM hundreds of alumni have started churches and missions in many parts of the world.

Giving by Example

What if Mrs. Clapp had not taken the time to pray daily for George? What if she had not witnessed to him and encouraged him?

A whole generation of young people today is looking for examples. Believe me, they will find someone to imitate. If we as parents and concerned believers do not accept the challenge, our children will find someone else.

When our daughter, Sarah, was seven, she wanted to iron like her mother, so Gisela bought her a toy iron. But that was not what Sarah had in mind! She wanted to use an iron that got hot. That was the problem, of course. But finally Gisela began to teach her to iron, showing her how to be careful not to get burned, and Sarah caught on surprisingly quickly. Before long she was excited to be ironing her own school clothes.

Then Sarah wanted to chop vegetables with the big kitchen knife—again, like her mother. Finally Gisela, supervising her closely, let her chop carrots with a small paring knife, but she knew the bigger knife would come in time. Our little girl was learning by imitation.

The younger generation today is faced with a choice: to follow the Lord with all their hearts or to live for themselves like the rest of the world. One of the greatest tragedies parents can experience is watching their children make wrong choices. It grieves me that multitudes of kids today are headed down the wrong road. Why are they so attracted to the values of this world and show little or no interest in spiritual matters?

Perhaps for part of the answer we need to look at ourselves. As parents, youth leaders or simply friends, we in the Body of Christ need to present an example before our children that they will want to follow.

I will never forget my experience at a youth group meeting where I shared my heart with a sizable group of highschoolers and presented the challenge of world evangelization. As I closed the meeting, I appealed to them to consider the claims of Jesus and make a decision about His Lordship in their own lives. During a time of prayer, I asked for a show of hands from those who were ready to share the Lord's heart for the world by giving their lives to reach the lost. I was astounded to discover that not one single young man or woman was willing to make that commitment. No one even spoke to me afterward.

I soon got a clue as to why those young people were so indifferent to the claims of Christ on their lives.

Following the meeting, the youth director offered to drive me back to my room. He led me out into the parking lot to his luxurious sports car. As I sank into the rich leather seat, I was enveloped with loud music coming from the high-tech tape-player. The dashboard and controls reminded me of an airplane cockpit. We took off like a rocket.

"Don't worry," he smiled. "I have everything under control."

But as we proceeded to zoom down the road, I was not so sure. I felt ill at ease for a reason that had nothing to do with our speed.

A single young man in his late twenties, the youth director chatted amiably with me about his career goals and plans. His remarks were sometimes serious, sometimes filled with ridicule—a mixture of flesh and Spirit that contradicted each other from one moment to the next. Our conversation did not reassure me that he understood about surrender to Christ or the importance of a personal devotional and prayer life.

Then I realized the main reason the youth of this church were so indifferent to the things of God. Here was a youth director who was barely more mature in the Lord than the young people he was hired to lead.

That young man was undoubtedly chosen by the church leadership because he was popular with the youth. He planned a full round of social activities for them and kept them busy all the time. I am sure the parents and leadership of the church reasoned that this young man was earning the respect of the youth. They probably believed he had many chances to talk to them about the things of the Lord.

But what kind of witness and example did he offer? His pattern of life, as far as I could tell from my brief time at the church, was committed not to the things of God but to the ways of the world.

The Law of Spiritual Reproduction

Most youth directors, I am sure, are not like this young man. I thank God for those who have taken their call seriously and are serving as unto the Lord. But the most basic rule in the propagation of any species—and in discipleship as well—is that *like begets like*.

Unfortunately, it does not take many hours of traveling to come across parents, pastors, youth directors and others in leadership who practice a worldly lifestyle before multitudes of children and young people, who are soaking up their example like sponges.

One young man in particular comes to mind. Let's call him John. His story is true. What happened to him occurs too often in our churches today.

As a high school student he heard the call for world evangelization at a summer youth camp. He came home and announced to his churchgoing parents that he was giving his life for missions. For a while they did not treat his new vision for the world too seriously. They were impressed by his newfound zeal for the Lord but were certain he would give up the idea in time.

But John didn't grow out of it—at least not at first. As he approached his final year in high school, he began ordering information not from respectable colleges but from Bible schools. His parents started to panic. Was he really thinking of going to one of those unaccredited institutes? What good would that do him in the real world?

So John's parents met with their pastor and asked him to help their son see that he was throwing his life away by thinking about full-time missions. The pastor agreed to meet with John and invited him over to his office for career counseling.

"You know, John," the pastor told him gently, "I was just like you when I first heard the call to the ministry. In fact, at first I wanted to go into missions, too. But I learned—

and you will, too—that if God is really calling you to do something like that, there's plenty of time. Your mom and dad are right to be concerned that you get a good education first. If your missionary service doesn't work out for one reason or another, then you'll always have something secure to fall back on."

The pastor went on to stress family concerns: "Have you thought about your future wife and the children you may someday have? Have you given any consideration to the emotional and physical adjustments they would have to make to a harsher way of life?"

Then the pastor explained some of the other risks and dangers involved in a missions career, pointing to the diplomas hanging on his own walls. "Get a good education first, John. I suggest you enroll in the best liberal arts college you can. Then, if you're really serious, you can go on to a good seminary and get your master's of divinity, or even a doctorate. You also need some experience working in our churches here at home. I have connections in other churches, and you can count on me to help you. Then, if you still want to go into missions, you'll know it's the real thing."

It made sense to John. Everyone he knew was giving him the same sort of "slow down" advice. Besides, his girlfriend's parents were opposed to the idea of his becoming a missionary. They were respectable people and did not want their daughter to have just a Bible school education or marry someone who did not have "a regular job." John figured that if he went to college first, she could enroll, too, with the help of her family, and the two would not have to be separated. He also figured this would give her some time to see how important the missions call was on his life.

John wrote to several missions organizations that year, since he was still planning to go overseas for short-term missions work as a summer volunteer. But after a year on campus he decided to switch to a business major. Everyone said that was where the future was in society. After that he never found the time to go overseas, not even short-term.

His girlfriend soon enrolled at the same college. They married when she was in her third year. Two years later the marriage ended in bitter divorce.

John's parents were heartbroken and realized that their interference had taken their son away from God's plan for his life and put him on a fast track to nowhere—at least nowhere for the Kingdom of God. But by then John was already pursuing a graduate degree. There was no more talk of the Lord and the mission field now; he was too busy sending his résumé to top business firms.

Today John is in a successful business, remarried and building a comfortable life for his family, complete with debt, a lavishly furnished house, two cars and a boat. To pay the bills, both he and his wife work. He still claims to be born again and attends church when it does not interfere with his career.

Where Do Things Go Wrong?

In our churches today we find millions of men and women just like John. In their young, formative years they heard the call of God on their lives but were not given the direction they needed to respond properly.

There is no guarantee, of course, that without his parents' intervention John would have gone into missions. It is futile to ask, "What if?" Yet still I wonder. Perhaps John's burden for the lost would have resulted in his staying home after all and becoming a sender rather than a goer.

But today John is neither.

The world is ready to offer substitutes to our children: security, prestige, wealth, power—and ineffectiveness for the Kingdom of God. But it does not have to be that way.

Where do things go wrong? They go wrong in our churches and youth group meetings, but first they go wrong in our homes. *If we model for our children a lifestyle that is consistent with what we believe, I assure you we can reach the next generation for Christ.*

As we walked across the grounds of a Hindu temple, our son Daniel, only three at the time, was attracted to a baby girl crawling around on the stones. He tried to take a picture of her with his toy camera. Instead, we placed them side by side and took a picture of them together with our real camera.

As I look at that picture today, I notice not only the little girl's torn and dirty dress but an amulet tied around her neck with a string. Her parents were Hindus; the amulet was to protect her from evil spirits.

Today I look at my children and am amazed how much they have grown. How fast time has flown since the days when they toddled around the house! Gisela and I love them dearly, and there is no doubt we want the very best for them.

Those Hindu parents loved their little girl as well and wanted the best for her. Unfortunately, the best they knew was an amulet to ward off evil spirits. They did not know that all the evil in the world has already been defeated at the cross, and that Christ died and rose again so that all might be saved.

More than half the population of India is made up of children under the age of sixteen. The little girl we saw that day is one of millions of children who may never hear about Jesus before they die.

I tell you this in all seriousness: What you and I give to our children today will determine what they and future generations will receive.

Imparting God's Heart to Our Children

In light of this reality, I want to offer five suggestions that will help you impart a burden for the lost world to the children and young people in your life. Your life, rather than your words, will be their greatest teacher.

Teach them from early on to love Jesus above all others. We expect certain routine things from our children. We expect them to bathe, brush their teeth, go to school, do their homework. These are not unreasonable demands; we see them as a basic part of living.

But when it comes to prayer and spiritual things, we slack up a bit. After all, we do not want to force our children into legalism or bondage. What we fail to realize is that making Jesus part of a child's everyday life is even more basic to living than learning to brush your teeth!

My daughter, Sarah, had an opportunity to experience this recently. To her dismay she found a wart growing on her arm. It showed no signs of stopping and embarrassed her terribly. She began to wear a Band-Aid over the wart to cover it up.

Gisela sat down with her one day.

"Sarah," she said, "I want to tell you something. Jesus is the same yesterday, today and forever. Jesus healed people before and He can heal us now. He answers prayer—you know that, Sarah. He has answered many of *your* prayers."

"Yes, Mommy, I know," Sarah replied. "But this?"

"Sarah, Jesus can answer your prayer and take your wart away, too."

"You really mean that, Mommy?"

"Yes, Sarah, I really mean that."

So Gisela and Sarah prayed together and asked Jesus to remove the wart from Sarah's arm.

"Sarah," Gisela told her, "from today on you will begin to see that wart getting smaller and smaller. Soon it will dry up and fall off."

So they began to watch Sarah's arm day after day and saw the wart shrivel up slowly in answer to their prayer.

A few weeks later I was in my study working on something when Gisela came in. Sarah followed with a shy grin on her face.

"Sarah," her mother said, "why don't you tell Daddy what happened?"

Sarah rolled up her sleeve, smiling even bigger. The wart had disappeared! Jesus had answered her prayer.

What a wonderful way for her to see that Jesus is interested in every part of our lives! When your children ask you for new clothes or the newest style of shoes, take the opportunity to say, "Why don't we ask Jesus about it?" Teach them to take their requests and desires to Him. If our children learn from the start to put Jesus before everything and everyone, they will pray about decisions and come to Him with the smallest request or concern. And later they will be freed from impure relationships and ungodly marriages.

We looked already at Jesus' words from Luke 14:26: "If anyone comes to me and does not hate his father and mother, his wife and children, his brothers and sisters—yes, even his own life—he cannot be my disciple." Let nothing come between your children and their relationship with Jesus.

Teach your children to die to themselves. Daniel had been eyeing a special toy for quite some time. He had finally saved up enough money, and it was only a matter of going to the store and making the purchase. But he came to me and said, "Daddy, I decided not to buy that toy."

"Why, Daniel?" I asked, puzzled.

"Last night after you prayed with me, I thought about the toy, and I thought about the thousands of people in India who don't have a Bible. I want my money to go to buy Bibles to give to those people."

Why did my son make a choice like that? Neither Gisela nor I forced him into that decision. It was simply because, by the grace of God, he had seen in our lives what we believed and lived for.

"If anyone would come after me," Jesus said, "he must deny himself and take up his cross and follow me" (Matthew 16:24). Jesus made it clear that death to our dreams, hopes, expectations and fears is the qualification for any Christian.

There is an unwritten rule in today's society, by contrast, that if we let our children face the disappointments and dashed hopes that come in this world, we must be poor parents. Even in the Christian subculture we are taught to push our children to make goals and meet them, to pursue dreams and satisfy the desires of a fleshly heart.

But what does Jesus ask of us? To die to it all. He does not want us to fit Him into our busy schedules. He wants us to come to Him without plans, goals or agendas but with an open calendar, an open life, ready for Him to arrange our schedule as He sees fit in the work of the Kingdom.

Did you know that pursuing the values set by our culture is a learned attitude? We can teach our children to unlearn those values as well. Or we can provide an atmosphere at home in which they never learn them in the first place. When children see their parents approach each day with a fresh dependence on the Lord for their plans and hopes, they, too, will learn to take up their cross daily.

Teach your children to forsake all. "Any of you who does not give up everything he has cannot be my disciple," said Jesus (Luke 14:33).

In a world dominated by ever-increasing materialism, no command seems harder to accept than this one. Citizens of some of the most affluent nations in the history of the human race still cannot be satisfied with what they have. We live in an age in which the acquisition of wealth and financial security has become a national pastime. But the love of material goods—including clothing, homes, insurance, properties, automobiles, even recreational toys—is one of the greatest hindrances to world evangelism.

Our attitude as parents and leaders will influence how our children see the "things" that everyone else runs after. Jesus asks us to forsake all if we want to follow Him. But before our children are able to do so, we must set the example.

Teach them to live a life of discipleship. For many, being born again is the end of their spiritual life, not the beginning. Many fail to understand—and fail to teach their children—that the Christian walk is an ongoing experience of daily submission to the Lord.

Walking with Jesus is not an easy road. He calls us to follow in His footsteps—but He was mocked, beaten and ultimately killed. Unless children and young people learn early on what this means, they will be blown away when the first fiery trial of their faith comes. These realities of the Christian life are taught on every page of the New Testament, but somehow we have managed to lock them away.

Young people who are serious about following Jesus need to understand that persecution and misunderstanding come to those who put Christ first. Suffering comes with the job. Sacrifice will always be needed if we are to reach the unreached with the Gospel.

I do an enormous amount of traveling. This means, of course, that I am often gone from home, and Gisela bears much of the responsibility for parenting Daniel and Sarah. To this day my children have never heard their mother grumble about my being gone. When they are sad or when they complain themselves, she draws them close and says, "It's our privilege to send Daddy out so that Jesus can use him to help reach the lost."

While we all feel the pain of this sacrifice Gisela and I have chosen to make, my children are not bitter.

Train your children to witness and share with others about Jesus. Young people can develop a burden for the lost at an early age simply by reaching out to those around them who do not know the Lord. They can learn to reach out to friends at school and in the neighborhood. They can work with the deacons in your church to call on the sick, become involved in prison ministries and visit those who are in need. They can accompany parents or youth leaders on short-term mission trips to nearby needy areas.

But remember, the best training for witnessing comes from you. As they observe you in your daily life, interacting with unsaved neighbors and friends, your children will learn to share the love of Jesus as well.

Make good use of available resources and materials. Obtain a world map and put it up in a prominent location in your home. Begin to pray as a family for missionaries you know about. Ask the Lord to direct your giving. Read together from missionary biographies. There are numerous wonderful volumes available on the lives of men and women like Amy Carmichael, Jim Elliot, Sadhu Sundar Singh, Hudson Taylor, William Carey and many others. Books like *Operation World* list prayer needs for each country of the world. The children's version of this wonderful book, titled *You Can Change the World*, is another excellent tool. Encourage your children to pray personally for a specific country or ethnic group.

Obtain the names and addresses of the missionaries your church supports. Make it a family project to learn about the countries they live and work in. Learn as much about their lives and needs as possible. Take the opportunity to invite visiting missionaries to your home. Gather your children around you and encourage them to ask as many questions as possible. Above all, pray for those missionaries.

Don't Let Them Miss Out

The other day Daniel was getting ready to go with some of his friends to a free Christian music concert. He was not planning to take any money, but when I heard it was free I told him, "Son, you should at least take five dollars for the offering. It may be free to you, but someone has to pay for it."

Then I added, "Daniel, maybe you should take a little more money, too, in case you find a T-shirt, or in case of an emergency."

My son's response stopped me in my tracks.

"Daddy," he said, "I don't want to take any more money. I'm not going to buy anything. I know other kids buy those things, but it's just a waste of my money—I don't want it."

I knew, since I know Daniel, that his statement was not a casual one.

Don't underestimate your children's ability to understand the reality of the lost world. Give them the opportunity to experience what you are living for. Live your life before them, coming to the Lord daily and depending on His strength and grace to be an example they will follow and imitate. Commit yourself to praying daily for your children, that the Lord will save them and call them to serve Him.

There is an abundance of material things that we can give to our children. But these are as useless as the amulet tied around that little girl's neck. The best thing we can give them is Jesus. Teach your children about His love and His heart. Teach them to follow Him, to lay down their lives to reach the lost. Don't let your children miss out on the best you can offer them.

Guidelines for Living in the Light of Eternity

As the plane began its final descent, flight attendants busied themselves picking up leftover cups, asking for tray tables to be put up and making sure we had our seatbelts fastened for landing. I found myself wondering what kind of people would be meeting me at the airport.

Tim and Rachel (not their real names) had called me a few months earlier with a startling statement.

"Brother K. P.," said Tim, "we want to give some money to your organization. But it's quite a large sum."

"How much are you talking about?" I asked him.

"A million dollars."

A million dollars! I had to ask again to make sure I had heard him right.

During the course of our conversation, I learned that Tim worked as an electrician while Rachel stayed at home to care for their children. I could not help but wonder how they were able to give this kind of money away.

"As a family," Tim said, "we live quite simply. The money we want to give is an inheritance."

"Is it all the money you have?" I asked.

"Yes, that's all of it," he answered.

"Tim, give me three days to pray about it," I said. "I'll call you back."

As I hung up, my heart was troubled. This young couple planned to give away all they had—everything—to our ministry. Their trust in us was sobering. Our need for responsibility and good stewardship weighed heavily on me.

I asked my staff to fast and pray with me about it. Three days later I called Tim back. I did not feel peace about taking the whole sum of money, I told him, but felt the Lord giving us the freedom to accept an amount needed for one specific project about which we had been praying—nearly $300,000. I also told him of other missions organizations he could contact and pray about helping, if God directed him to do so.

A few days later their check arrived in the mail.

Now I was scheduled to be in their area to speak at a missions conference and was about to meet Tim and Rachel.

They were at the gate, greeting me with warm smiles. Nothing they wore would reveal them as an obvious source of a million dollars. I hardly knew what to think, but already my preconceptions were being blown away.

After a warm handshake, Tim led the way to their car. Now I was really in for a shock! He loaded my luggage into the back of an old, well-used station wagon, and off we drove.

Their house was not grandiose by any stretch of the imagination, but Rachel was a gracious hostess and their troop of small children played happily and noisily throughout the house.

As I spent more time with Tim and Rachel, I came to know their story. As a young, single man, Tim had spent much time with the Lord in prayer and in the Word. He became so moved with compassion for the lost world that it nearly broke his heart. He sold his house, cars and most of his clothes, took the money and sent it off quietly to many different countries for the printing of Gospel literature. He lived so radically for Jesus that some people actually thought he had gone crazy.

During this time he met Rachel. Before long they were in love. But Rachel came from a rich family.

"Even though I love you," Tim told her, "I can't even think about marrying you."

"Why not?"

"You know I've given my life, my job, everything for one cause—to win the lost for the Lord. If I marry you, with the millions of dollars that come with your name, you may not want to live the life I have chosen. I *can't* marry you, Rachel."

"You don't understand. I love you because of the way you are. That's the kind of life I want, too."

So they made a pledge between themselves and the Lord: They would never touch a penny of the money Rachel would bring to their marriage. Tim would continue his electrician's job to meet their basic needs. They would live as simply as possible, buying used clothing and driving used cars. And all the money from Rachel's inheritance, as well as any extra money from Tim's job, would go completely to the Lord's work.

I will never forget Tim and Rachel, their house, their car and the lifestyle they choose to live. I will never forget the look of complete contentment and joy I saw on their faces. Every day they evaluate their lives, asking themselves if their actions, decisions and purchases are helping to reach the lost.

Their lives represent a choice to live and interpret everything in the light of eternity.

Becoming More Eternally Minded

Over the years I have heard many discussions on world evangelization. It is interesting to meet with others who share similar and differing viewpoints. But when the discussions involve the issue of living with less, they often take a philosophical turn and offer little practical application.

We can debate practical theology if we want to while millions are plunging into hell, but we must understand one thing about scaling down our lifestyles: One hundred years from now, what will remain? Houses, money, plans, buildings—these will no longer have any meaning. We must adjust our lifestyles *now* and invest our lives to reach the lost world.

During World War II the people of England scaled down their lifestyles to the barest of essentials. They knew that if they did not commit themselves fully to winning the war, they might lose everything. So they gladly gave money, gold, silver, even their young men for the cause.

Many believers are searching for reality in their lives. They want some way to connect what they believe with what they live, but they do not quite know what steps to take. How *do* we implement the call of eternity into our lives? How do we become more missions-conscious and begin to live more simply?

There are two dangers we must be careful to avoid. First, we can take the message of the Gospel and translate it into *all action and no heart*. We can get whipped up into a frenzy of activity and supposed sacrifice that means nothing at all because it is not motivated by love. Second, we can see the life Jesus asks us to live and become overwhelmed by what seem to be impossible demands. The result is *no action at all*; doing something is just too hard.

The problem with you and me and the culture in which we are immersed is that we are taught the self-help approach to spiritual living. Instead of taking the Bible at face value, we are taught to find Scriptures that justify our need for happiness and more comfortable lives. We are no longer centering on Jesus and His will but using Him as a means to comfort in the here-and-now. We even take what the world offers us and put labels on it to "Christianize" it, whether it be heavy-metal music, color-coordination seminars or aerobic videos. We have allowed ourselves to be deceived by our society and the opinions of others.

One man's comment in a church recently gave me insight into the workings of human nature.

"I'm a medical doctor," he said. "If I were to live the lifestyle you preach about, I wouldn't be able to keep my practice. I own a home and a car. If I were to reduce my standard of living as you suggest, my colleagues wouldn't take me seriously anymore. I don't even think they'd want to come into my house. If I'm to be accepted in the medical community, I have to live this lifestyle."

Did I detect some self-justification? But arguing with him was not the answer.

"All I can offer are some basic guidelines," I responded. "You have to work it out in your own life."

I hope the following seven guidelines will help to make *your* way clear as you seek the Lord for living in the light of eternity.

1. Go to the Word of God

Any issue that falls into the realm of obedience to the Lord must be found in His Word. As you commit to opening your heart to the Word of God every day, the Holy Spirit will take what you are reading and make personal application.

2. Apply the Word of God

Apply truths from the Word of God to your own practical realm. Determine to take the Word of God personally. Ask yourself, *How does this apply to me specifically—
where I am now and in regard to those with whom I live and
work?*

Jesus said, "If anyone would come after me, he must deny
himself and take up his cross and follow me" (Matthew
16:24). Now ask yourself, *What does it mean to deny myself
and take up my cross today?* Wait before the Lord and ask
the Holy Spirit to reveal His truth to you.

Obedience to the Lord, I have found, is seldom a pleas-
ant experience for my flesh. Most of the time I do not enjoy
it!

A friend of mine shared once that he was setting his
alarm clock a few minutes earlier in the morning in order
to get up to pray.

How he hated that alarm clock! A few times he really
pounded it, he told me, to shut the thing off. Sometimes
he buried his head in the pillow and went back to sleep.
When he did get up, he shuffled to the sink and splashed
cold water on his face. (He hated that cold water, too!)
And as he knelt by the bed to pray, that did not feel good
either.

Then, he told me with a chuckle, he began to realize
that it was working—he *was* waking up. His prayers *were*
being answered. And he was drawing closer to the Lord.

We are not ethereal, spirit-like vapors living in plastic
shells. We are made of flesh and bone. When we look at
the cross where Jesus died, we see agony, misunderstanding, loneliness, rejection, humiliation, loss and death.
When the Lord asks us to take up the cross, to understand
Christ and His fullness, we must personally accept inconveniences in our lives. It may mean fasting and praying,
spending a long time in the Lord's presence, rejecting the

urge to buy an expensive shirt, gathering the courage to tell someone about the Lord.

Your mind may argue with you and try to rationalize this all away. Your emotions may protest the discomfort you have accepted. But deep within your heart, you know that the Word of God is true and that, to obey it, you must apply it to your life.

3. Implement Decisions Now

Take the actions and decisions you know are right and implement them in your life right now. Do not wait for some big revelation to appear to you in the night sky. Right now begin to sacrifice, pray, fast, witness, repent, ask for forgiveness from others when you wrong them—whatever you know God has told you to do.

As you walk with Him, He will reveal more truths to you and shed more light on your path. (The place to begin, as I said, is the Word of God.) But start right now to implement the meaning of the cross in your life.

We are all at different places in our walks with the Lord. Something the Lord has called me to deny in my life may mean nothing to you. What you must do is take the knowledge the Lord has given *you* and do what you know to be the right thing.

4. Say No to Your Culture

Whenever the culture around you hinders your obedience to the voice of God and what He has shown you in His Word, say no to it, no matter how impossible this seems.

Daniel and his friends were taken captive into Babylon and offered the king's rich food as their daily provision. It was considered an honor to eat the king's food and drink his wine. (The first portion of both had been offered on a pagan altar, and animals were used that were ceremonially unclean.) Daniel had every reason to say to himself, *I'm in Babylon now, and my captivity has not happened without God's knowledge. There's nothing wrong with eating and drinking what is set before me.*

But Daniel had a revelation that went beyond the culture in which he lived, and he chose to remain true to what God had revealed rather than to the culture. "Daniel resolved not to defile himself. . ." (Daniel 1:8).

We must not conform to our culture if our obedience to the Lord is jeopardized in the process. We, and not the culture in which we live, bear the responsibility for our walk with the Lord.

At the same time, every culture perceives needs differently. In India, for example, you rarely see pews or chairs in a local church. We sit on the floor to worship; it is part of the culture. In the West we sit in pews or on chairs; again, it is part of the culture. Floors or pews—neither is more spiritual; it is simply a matter of culture.

Imagine for a moment that the leadership of a Western church decides that regular pews are not good enough but must be replaced with individual, cushioned, reclining rockers for more comfort. Now, that does seem a little outrageous! There is nothing wrong with worshiping God sitting in a pew, but there is no need to squander money on new seating when it can better be used to further the work of the Lord.

We must learn to distinguish between the dictates of culture and what the Lord is asking of us.

5. Be Persuaded in Your Heart

Ultimately each of us must be persuaded in our own heart and begin to move and act where we are. Nowhere does the Bible say that all-out commitment to Christ means we have to take our family to some remote jungle area and die there. The call of the Lord is different for each individual.

One day you will stand before the Lord and be called to give an account for the things He asked you to do.

The native missionaries who labor on the mission field are there because they heard God's voice telling them to go. They knew the troubles and trials before them. They saw the need, heard the call and obeyed.

We must live in the same reality. When we hear God's voice, we must act accordingly and do whatever it is He is asking us to do. A multimillionaire who owns a huge business may be more committed to Christ than a pastor who lives in a hovel. You must be persuaded in your own conscience that you are following the Lord's direction for your life.

As a matter of fact, it may be more difficult to stay behind as a sender than go yourself. You are not on the front lines. You are living simply, working a regular job, remaining faithful to the Lord and preserving your testimony before all your coworkers. Taking the money you earn and giving it faithfully to support a missionary in China or India or Bangladesh—someone you have never seen for whom you are also praying—is true sacrifice and living by faith.

No one can dictate to you a certain standard of living or draw any kind of line, culture or no culture. Each of us must be persuaded to live before the Lord as we are led by Him.

6. Don't Be Motivated by Guilt

Let no one intimidate you or condemn your actions. Check yourself if you hear yourself thinking thoughts like *I'd be a better Christian if I did this or that* or *I feel bad about the house [or car] I own*.

If you are motivated to do something out of guilt, don't do it! God is not in the business of putting people on guilt trips to make them do something. He will call you on the carpet and ask you, with love, "Are you living by My standards?" But He will never condemn you.

When Jesus spoke to Peter after His resurrection, He did not say (as we might have been tempted), "You creep, I can't believe you denied Me! I'm going to get you now." No, from just one glance Peter could tell that Jesus was saying something very different: "Peter, I love you more than you could ever know. Forget the past—everything is forgiven. Now go and feed My sheep."

Whatever you hear, whatever you read, whatever challenges you—remember that your resulting actions should never be generated by guilt, which is carnality. Purpose in your heart that you will never live by someone else's standard, but only by the principles you know to be true from the Word of God, and by the Holy Spirit teaching you daily as you are open to His leading in your life.

7. Guard Against False Humility

Be on your guard for false humility (which is actually pride) and condemning anyone else. It is easy to read a book like this and think of "So-and-So, who really needs to hear this message!" It is always easier to see the speck in someone else's eye than the beam in your own. But remember Jesus' sober warning: "Do not judge, or you too will be judged. For in the same way you judge others, you will be judged, and with the measure you use, it will be measured to you" (Matthew 7:1–2).

No one can live a life that will satisfy everyone. We cannot be motivated to make changes in our lives simply because they will make us look good in our friends' eyes or because they will make our friends look bad. Pride can drive us to do stupid, unreasonable and downright sinful things.

How grateful I am for the staff God has given us at our Gospel for Asia headquarters in Texas! To describe our relationship I would use the word *family*. Our work and lives are closely intertwined. We agonize for one another in prayer, come to one another's aid during struggles and rejoice together in victories, both in our own lives and on the field.

It would be easy to begin comparing lifestyles, salaries and convictions. To a certain extent that is the temptation among any group of Christians. But we must remember that our commitment to one another goes beyond the eight-to-five workday. We all serve the same Master. We all have love for one another. And we all live with the same profound commitment to see the lost reached. Everything else is incidental.

We cannot expect each other to be perfect. We must keep our own consciences and walks with the Lord pure, before both God and man. If we are following God's Word, we have no reason to fear condemnation from others, nor will we desire to lord it over others as if we were more spiritual.

Picking Up Your Cross

Sometimes after I speak in a meeting, I feel troubled about what I said. *Perhaps I was too strong,* I think. *Perhaps I made people feel guilty and will drive them to legalistic bondage.*

But this is not my motivation. My only desire is to stir up hearts to see the reality beyond our own narrow horizons. A world out there is dying and going to hell. All the Lord has asked me to do is share His heart and give some practical guidelines for becoming involved in His work—which I have tried to do.

Someday we will all stand before Him. Each of us is responsible individually for what we do with this information. Will we ignore it, like the nagging alarm clock that wakes us up too early in the morning? Or will we do our part to help reach our generation for Christ?

You are the one who has to live with yourself and the decisions you make.

What Will You Do?

As I travel around North America, speaking in churches and home groups, I have learned that it is valuable to close my message with a time of questions and answers. Not only does my audience have a chance to ask questions or share what is on their hearts, but I am provided with a wealth of information on the state of the Church at large.

On one such occasion in California, a young man stood up to ask a question. He was a university student searching for answers.

"I just finished reading your book *Road to Reality*," he said. "You say some hard things in that book. What I want to know is, how can I live out these principles that you talk about? I find it pretty hard to walk away from the comfortable life I am so accustomed to living. Can you help me?"

As he spoke, I was already praying, *Lord, give me some way to answer this young man.*

"Your questions tell me something about you," I told him. "You are troubled. You want desperately to do the right thing. You don't know what to do with this message or how to apply it. You know Jesus is asking you to sell out for Him, but you're looking for some emotional confirmation, some happiness to support your thinking. But you aren't finding any, are you?"

There was absolute silence in the auditorium. I realized this young student was really the spokesperson that day for many others facing the same struggle.

You may be facing this struggle, too. How will you apply the guidelines we have talked about?

Walking Away from the World

The stories of Abraham and Moses offer practical help as we consider paring down our lifestyles.

Longing for a Better Country

I was browsing through a book on ancient culture recently with some fascinating insights into the city where Abraham came from. Sir Leonard Woolley, a British archaeologist, traveled to Mesopotamia in the 1920s and studied the ancient city of Ur. Through many excavations Woolley and his colleagues learned that Ur was a very affluent society, a bustling port city through which many luxury goods traded hands, including precious stones, gold, timber and ivory.

Abram (as his name was then) lived in the midst of this affluence, surrounded by his family and relatives. Ur was his hometown. His life was secure and comfortable. Yet he was different from those around him in one significant way. Everyone else was involved in heathen worship, while Abram had a relationship with the living God.

One day God appeared to him and said, "Abram, I want you to leave your father, mother, brothers, sisters, relatives, land—everything."

Imagine what it must have been like for Abram to hear *that!*

"Then what, God? Where do You want me to go?"

"I'll show you."

Leave everything? Even my parents? Abram's thoughts whirled in his mind. *How can my family even begin to understand something like this? First of all, I worship a God who talks to me. They'll think my mind is gone. Besides, family ties here are deeply ingrained. They'll think I have no respect for them.*

Abram spent days wrestling with the call of God. What the Almighty had asked him to do was not easy. It went against everything Abram had been taught to value from childhood. It went against the very fiber of the community and culture.

We have the advantage of knowing the rest of the story, of course, while Abram and those around him had no idea what was going to happen. There was no story in Genesis in which to discover the happy ending.

One evening at dinner Abram was unusually subdued. His face, pale and drawn, showed the strains of his inner struggle. It did not go unnoticed.

"What's wrong, Abe?" asked his father, Terah. "You haven't been yourself tonight—or lately, for that matter. Something's on your mind."

Abram swallowed. His mind was made up. It was time to tell them.

"Father, I'm leaving."

The words hung in the air and seemed to echo again and again in the heavy silence that followed.

Finally Terah spoke. "You're—leaving? Where are you going?"

All eyes were on Abram as they waited for his reply.

"I'm sorry, Father—I just can't tell you. You wouldn't understand. All I know is that the God I worship has called me to leave everything here and follow Him. Would you please excuse me?"

Abram rose and walked out into the night air, glad for some relief from the intense atmosphere.

His relatives and friends discussed Abram's announcement late into the night.

"The man has no respect for his parents, I'll tell you that much!" steamed one.

"Abe is no dummy," said another. "I think he must've found a better place than Ur where he can strike it rich. That's why he won't tell us!"

"No, something is troubling him—you can see that plainly," a third responded. "And he mentioned this God—which one does he mean? And have you heard that this God talks? Abram says so. It makes me wonder if he isn't plagued with hallucinations."

"We'll have more time with him tomorrow," Terah broke in. "Let's all get some sleep tonight."

Obviously to obey the call of God would have serious ramifications.

How *could* Abram walk away from Ur, from wealth and security and comfort, from his family and friends and home and wealth? For the rest of his life, we are told, he lived in tents in a strange country—a pilgrim on the face of the earth.

We find the answer in Hebrews 11:10: "He was looking forward to the city with foundations, whose architect and builder is God."

A little later in his life, when Abraham parted ways with his nephew, he allowed Lot to choose the most fertile pastureland to settle in. I am sure Lot and his wife danced for joy at the sight of all they now owned. And I wonder what Abraham was thinking as he walked away.

Later the Lord came to him and said, "Abraham, look up into the night sky. Do you see the stars there? I said just one word and they all came into being. So shall your descendants be, Abraham. I am your reward."

Did Abraham know that Ur, the city of wealth and prosperity that he willingly left behind, would one day crumble into dust and be buried under the shifting desert sands? Did he know that thousands of years later some British archaeologist would bring his shovel and rediscover Ur with all of its gold and silver?

Obviously Abraham knew nothing of what was to come. But he knew one thing: There was a much better place on which he set his sights. He, along with the other men and women of faith,

> were longing for a better country—a heavenly one. Therefore God is not ashamed to be called their God, for he has prepared a city for them. . . . For here we do not have an enduring city, but we are looking for the city that is to come.
>
> Hebrews 11:16; 13:14

Seeing Him Who Is Invisible

Then there is Moses and the life of luxury he willingly left behind in Egypt. Moses was raised in Pharaoh's courts as a prince. He had education, influence, power and wealth at his disposal. Yet he chose to walk away from it all.

Moses would have been more justified than the rest of the Hebrews in wanting the good things of Egypt—the tasty food, the comforts and the securities—for he had experienced them all to the fullest. When you think about his decision from a logical frame of reference, it makes no sense. I am sure those around him felt the same way. Perhaps some of the Hebrew slaves said to him, "What are you doing, Moses? Don't you realize you could be the key to our freedom? Just lie low. Don't rock the boat. Stay in the palace and someday soon we'll overthrow all these Egyptians."

But Moses walked away from the luxury and privileges and chose to become a shepherd.

How could he give up all he had? Again we find the answer in Hebrews: "[Moses] saw him who is invisible" (Hebrews 11:27).

Years later as Moses led the people of Israel through the desert and endured years of hardship along the journey, what kept him going? He could say, "I have seen Him who is invisible." He remained faithful, following the cloud by day and the fire by night. He lived a life that looked beyond the pleasures of his day and focused on the eternal I AM.

The reason Abraham and Moses could walk away from this world and all its enticements was that they saw something that others could not. Eternity was stamped upon their eyes.

"You've Been a Long Time Coming"

One evening not too long ago, I sat alone in a hotel room. The next day I would be speaking in a missions conference about living with the reality of a lost world. It was late and I was tired. But instead of praying about the next day or going to bed as I should have, I switched on the television. An episode of "Star Trek" was just beginning.

Now, I must explain to you that I have always been fascinated by the futuristic gadgets this show portrays! So I sat back and watched it from beginning to end.

As I turned off the TV, I looked at my watch. It was 11:30 and I was exhausted.

I can't believe I did that! I said to myself. *I have to get up early and speak tomorrow.*

I had wasted a precious hour that I should have used either praying or sleeping. Jesus stayed up all night, but He was praying! My body is not made of steel and I wear out if I try to go on just a few hours' sleep each night. I was disappointed in myself.

Then I realized the devil was using my mistake to waste even more of my time as I sat and wallowed in guilt and frustration.

I knelt quickly beside my bed, buried my head in the pillow and said, "Jesus, I know Your blood is sufficient to forgive me and cleanse me from my wrongdoing. Will You please do it?"

The accusing voice of the enemy whispered into my mind, *Are you stupid? How many times have you said that before?*

But I knew in my heart I had been forgiven.

"One more time," I said. "Jesus said He would do it."

I went to bed with peace of mind and heart. I fell asleep quickly and woke the next morning feeling fresh and grateful for a brand-new day that Jesus and I would go through together.

My dear friend, we must make new decisions every day with the knowledge that this is a new day. We cannot mourn yesterday's losses or stand on yesterday's triumphs. Jesus told us that if we want to follow Him, we must take up our cross *daily*. As we continue to focus on eternity, we must allow ourselves to be crucified every day. As we do, we will see our human nature in its true state and see the need around us.

I heard a story someplace from the pre–Civil War days of the South, when sanitary conditions in certain places were poor. A plague came to one city and brought havoc. The city's death toll climbed; hardly a home did not have sorrow or a vacant room.

In one poor home, the disease came and did fast work. Each family member was carried out shrouded in a sheet, one after the other, until only the mother and her five-year-old son remained. He crept up into his mother's lap, his eyes serious.

"Mother," he said, "Father is dead. My brothers and sisters are dead. What if you die? What will I do?"

With that little face so close to hers, what could she say? She must be brave. She answered as quietly and calmly as she could, "My boy, if I should die, the Lord Jesus will come and take care of you."

That was quite satisfactory to him. The boy had been trained from his earliest years to know and love the Savior. He went back to playing on the floor.

It's all taken care of, he thought. *If Mother should die, Jesus will come, and that will be all right.*

His question proved prophetic. The disease reached his mother, and soon she was carried away as well. He followed and saw where she was buried, then came back to the house. In the midst of the hustle and bustle he was forgotten, left alone in the humble home.

He tried to sleep that night but could not, so he got up and dressed himself as best he could. He found his way to the cemetery where they had laid his mother. Finding the spot, he threw himself upon the fresh earth. Sleep came quickly.

Early the next morning a Christian gentleman was coming down the road from some errand of mercy that had kept him out all night. As he passed the graveyard he saw the boy, quickly imagining a heartbreaking story.

"My boy," he called out, "what are you doing here?"

The boy raised himself and rubbed his eyes. "Well, my father is dead. My brothers and sisters are dead. And now my mother is dead. But she said that if she died, Jesus would come for me. And He hasn't come. I'm tired of waiting."

The man swallowed hard and then said quickly, as he tried to control his voice, "Well, my boy, I have come for you."

The boy looked up at the gentleman with wide eyes and said, "You've been a long time coming."

As I write these words, there comes before my eyes a vision. This vision is with me day and night. It never goes away, and I do not want it to. The vision is of a great sea of faces from Africa, Turkey, Iran, the Middle East, Bhutan, Myanmar, Japan, China, India. In this great cloud of faces, eyes are searching and sad and cry out, "You've been a long time coming."

The fulfillment of this vision through world evangelization cannot be done by illusion or manipulating others to perform spiritual-looking tricks. World evangelization can be accomplished only by those who have abandoned their lives, obeying what Jesus said: "Forsake all and follow Me." It begins with an attitude of the heart.

Life is short. There is no sense investing our time, energy and finances in things that will soon burn up and be gone. Each morning as we awake, let's take a hard look at our lives in the light of eternity. We must ask ourselves, *What are the essentials that I can live with?*

Time is running out. Hell is real. Heaven is real. Soon it will be too late; we *must* reach our generation with the Gospel of Christ. World evangelism will be carried out by rational, sober-minded, unmovable soldiers of the cross. We are called to follow the example of Jesus, who fixed His eyes on the cross that was before Him and never turned to the right or to the left. Jesus' reason for living was reaping the harvest of souls.

The decision to live with the cross on a daily basis is a choice you must make. We read our newspapers, listen to the radio, watch TV and see every day before our eyes the poor, the unknown, the unheard millions who are dying. We respond in one of two ways. Either we choose to ignore what we see and know, or we take up our cross and follow Jesus.

My question to you is, How will *you* respond? It is your decision; no one can make it for you.

What Will You Do?

I heard Billy Graham say once that the hardest thing for a person to do is to give away his money. When I first heard that, I thought, *That statement makes no sense. How can that be?* But he went on to say that a person's money represents his ambitions, dreams, toil, priorities, time, activities, motives—everything. And it is hard for someone to give away his money without expecting a return here and now.

It is easy to justify our own needs and comforts. For that we seldom seek the counsel of the Lord. But when it comes to sacrificing and giving to extend God's Kingdom, we have to pray about it. What a contrast with the apostle Paul! When he gave his life to the Lord, one of the first questions out of his mouth was, "What shall I do, Lord?" (See Acts 9:6 KJV). This is the question we, too, must ask.

What went through your mind when you read Gisela's story back in chapter 4—the fourteen-year-old renouncing a comfortable life for the Kingdom? Perhaps it sounded extreme to you. Perhaps you had a hard time relating to her situation.

But giving your life to the Lord is a daily choice, a daily taking up of the cross. Every day we must say to Jesus, "Lord, today I am Yours. Body, soul, spirit, wealth, children, spouse—all that I have, all that I am, is Yours. What do You want me to do today? How do You want me to live?" Allow the Holy Spirit to take the Word of God and weave it into the very fiber of your being. Allow Him to guide you as you step out.

Perhaps you have had your eye on a new pair of shoes or a suit or maybe a new recliner for the living room. Can you say, "Lord, this money is Yours and my time is Yours. What do You want me to do?"

Then be still. Let the Lord speak to you.

Many years ago I went to a barber who cut my hair for twelve dollars, including the tip. That was a good sum of money at the time to spend on a haircut, but he always did a nice job. I knew of another place that did it for three bucks, but I always had the feeling they would butcher my hair.

At that time the Lord was teaching me this principle: *If one hair on your head that falls off is so important to Me, you should know that I am concerned about everything in your life. Is it too much for you to ask Me what you should do with even one dollar or one hour?*

I began to understand that bringing my life before the Lord was not an unbearable burden but a privilege. So I took some time and prayed to the Lord about my haircut.

"Lord," I prayed, "I have always made this decision with my rational mind. What do You want me to do?"

I considered my options; basically they boiled down to twelve dollars or three. God was giving me a choice to make in the light of eternity.

I decided to go to the butcher. (He was not, as it turned out, a butcher at all!)

It was simpler than I expected. God did not holler in my ear, "Go to this one!" But I did not have to hear an audible voice. Through the Holy Spirit, God speaks to us as clearly as He did in the days of the New Testament—not through beating us on the head but through giving us a choice. All we have to do is ask Him daily, "Lord, what do You want me to do?"

The Practical Application

Sometimes sincere people go forward in meetings, repent of their sins and surrender their lives to Jesus Christ. But when they walk away, nothing changes. Why not? *There is no practical application.*

I am asking that we begin to think in these terms: "My life, and all that I am, belongs to You, Lord." We need to take what we know is true and apply it to every area of our lives. The Lord is concerned about every decision we make.

It is my sincere prayer that as you come away from reading this book, the devil will not take these thoughts and "immunize" you so that your heart is hardened to change. Everything I write will mean nothing after you close this book unless you do something practical about it. The choices and decisions you make will affect the course of your life forever.

Some of you will sell your large house in order to purchase a smaller one and begin to live more simply. Some of you will sell your diamond rings and jewelry and give that money for missions.

Some of you will take the money you are saving for the future and say, "I will live by faith. There is nothing worse than death, and my life is not mine anyway—it's His."

Some of you will look at your job in a new light. It will no longer be the most important thing in your life but a means to help you do what you can, as you walk through this life, to extend God's Kingdom. One doctor tells me often, "The reason I'm a surgeon is simply that I know I can help support missionaries who are winning thousands to Jesus." A carpenter tells me, "The only reason I work so hard at my job is so I can support the work of the Lord."

Some of you will go to the mission field yourselves in obedience to the call of the Lord. You will choose to give up the comforts and conveniences that others enjoy, choosing to live in another culture so that others can hear the Gospel.

Perhaps God has spoken to your heart to begin to support one of these needy brothers or sisters. Or perhaps He is asking you to give up your job, your dream of a comfortable lifestyle, that girlfriend or boyfriend, and go to the mission field yourself, investing a significant portion of your life for those who have never heard the Gospel.

The opportunities to bring in the harvest are plenty. Right now millions in unreached lands are waiting to hear the Gospel and thousands of missionaries are willing and ready to go. I do not know which decisions you will make. There are many to be made. You must begin where you are with your eyes on Jesus. Sit back and consider what you have read. Take time to be quiet before the Lord and listen to His voice. The decisions you make must be rational and soberminded.

Then begin to implement God's call on your life now. Cut back on those unnecessary things in your life—the gum, the extra ice cream, the plans for buying another car. No, it does not feel good, but you are beginning to pick up the cross. You are answering the call of eternity. And the consequences of a decision like this will last forever.

You will not regret it, I guarantee you.

I cannot challenge you to do anything I have not done myself. When I began to make choices to live in the light of eternity, the Lord came to me with a sharp knife and said, "Son, here's the knife. You have to do the surgery on yourself. I can't do it for you."

You will struggle with uncertainty, self-pity and sorrow. You will face criticism and misunderstanding from others. We are strangers and pilgrims on the earth, just as Abraham and Moses were. But I know one thing: My eyes are fixed on eternity and the thousands of souls I want to bring with me. I do not compare my life with someone else's. I compare my life with Jesus' command: "Forsake all and follow Me." Jesus has never asked me to do something that He did not do. I will follow Him.

May the Holy Spirit give you the ability to see the vision of the faces of people crying out for life. May He give you His burden for souls who are perishing. Only He can tell you what you must do with your life, your time and your resources. All I can give you are examples and illustrations.

I pray that each day you will make time to get to know Him better and share His heart.

Recently I received two special letters from John and Sara.

"My mom and dad support some missionaries, so my sister and I decided to support a missionary," wrote John.

Sara added, "I am glad you have started this work. Please send us a missionary to pray for and support."

It blessed me to read their letters and know that these children are already beginning to invest their lives in eternity.

In my mind's eye, I look forward to that day when we will all see Jesus face to face. As believers from all times and places are united before His throne, we will offer Him the praise He is worthy to receive. John and Sara will be there. So will their mom and dad, and multitudes of others who laid down their lives for the sake of the Kingdom, whether by praying and sending others or by going themselves.

As we worship our Lord, others will join us, too—men and women from every tongue and tribe and nation, those for whom others prayed and gave and lived and even died. As we gather around God's throne, we will know beyond any doubt that no price was too high to pay to serve Jesus. It was worth it all.

In this final hour let us choose the cross and not turn back.

My Prayer

Lord Jesus, we thank You that in Your grace and mercy You forgive and cleanse us, that You pick us up and motivate us to continue on our journey with You.

Lord, we realize that we are not living in a neutral zone. We are living in the enemy's territory. The Bible tells us that the whole world lies in the lap of the wicked one. We are so aware, O Lord, that the god of this world is our enemy. We know that the more we seek to please You, the more we seek to do Your will, the more we pray, the more we reach out to the lost world, the more we accept the cross, the more we will be faced with the fiery darts of the evil one.

And Lord, it seems so often that the battleground is in our minds. How often—even daily—we face discouragement, questions, doubts, concerns, agonies, misunderstandings, self-pity. How often we find ourselves wanting to get out of the battle, to run off and hide somewhere! How often we find our hearts getting cold. We know it is part of the struggle we're in. We are soldiers who sometimes get wounded and hurt and have to lie low when the bullets come straight toward us.

Yet Lord, we know that whether we stand or fall, we are still in Your hands. Today we surrender our lives to You completely once again. We ask You to take absolute control of our hearts.

Thank You, Lord, for encouraging and motivating us. Thank You for Your love that fills our hearts. Thank You for giving us every weapon we need to continue in this warfare. Thank You for encouraging us and giving us peace. Thank You for filling our hearts with joy and giving us strength. Thank You for Your great salvation.

In Jesus' precious name, Amen.

If you care about the lost millions of Asia, would like a free one-year subscription to SEND! *The Voice of Native Missions* or are interested in learning more about the ministry of Gospel for Asia and the native missionary movement, contact:

Gospel for Asia
1932 Walnut Plaza
Carrollton, TX 75006

Or in Canada:

120 Lancing Dr., #6
Hamilton, Ont. L8W 3A1
Canada

1-800-WIN-ASIA (946-2742)
or (214) 416-0340